My Journey to Exodus

How My Pain Produced Promise

Collaborative Works by Extraordinary Women

My Journey to Exodus

How My Pain Produced Promise

Presented by
Xaviera L. Bell

Copyright © 2015 by Xaviera L. Bell
Cover Design: Keyona Simone (Kreativity by K.Sim)
ISBN: 978-0-99155419-5

All rights reserved. Reproduction or translation of any part of this book through any means without permission of the copyright owner in unlawful, except for promotional use by individual contributing authors or book reviewers who may quote passages in a review in print or online, as long as the following statement is included:

Excerpted from My Journey to Exodus: How My Pain Produced Promise

Request for other permissions or further information should be addressed in writing to:
Exodus_Project@outlook.com

Although every precaution has been taken in the preparation of this book, the publisher, the author, and the contributors assume no responsibility for errors or omissions. Liability will not be assumed for any damages resulting from the use of information contained herein.

PUBLISHER'S NOTE: This anthology is a work of true life testimonies. Each testimony is based on true life situations the author experienced or has personal knowledge of. Each author is individually responsible for any inaccuracies.

This book is dedicated to our mothers, our sisters, our daughters, our aunts, our cousins, and our friends.. This book is dedicate.. To Women…

Table of Contents

A Field of Tulips- 6
Angie B. Moree

Penetrating Innocence- 18
C.J. Lane

My David and Goliath Story- 34
Carol Evans Ryan

Openly Broken- 56
Candace Smith

The Vow That I Made.. To Me- 72
Dionne Brunson

Depression- 86
Candace Smith

Sticks and Stones- 90
D. Elaine Wiggins

What Glitters.. Isn't Always Gold- 102
Emily Hendrickson

Break Up To Make Up.. With Me- 114
Erica Ware

If I Knew Then- 122
Gina Perryman

Broken Pieces- 134
Itiah Lewis

My Paradox- 144
C.J. Lane

Happy Anniversary- 148
Jeanette Benjamin

If They Say So- 160
LaToya Perry

Keeping Secrets & Telling Lies- 174
Neema Campbell

The Spirit of Sabotage- 188
Minister Rose Shaw

Escape To Freedom- 206
Shadawn Parker

The Greatest Deception- 222
Xaviera L. Bell

Unbreakable- 228
Tanisha Grey

Standing in the Storms of Life- 244
Wryshona Isaac

Seven Times Hotter- 258
Xaviera L. Bell

A Field of Tulips

By: Angie B. Moree

Angie B. Moree

LOVE FOR THE NATIONS FOUNDER
BEL EKRI PUBLISHING
CO-FOUNDER

myloveforthenations@gmail.com
www.loveforthenations.com
www.belekripublishing.com

To judge a book by the cover never does the reader any justice. For so long my past was like a dark storm cloud that covered my life with only glimpses of sunlight. Those who were in my circle watched closely to see if clear skies would be the forecast for the day. Throughout my time of turbulence I learned that no matter how bad things in your life get or how much you feel you have failed in some situations, there are those who are depending on you to survive.

I developed a keen sense of purpose and love for myself and only desire to see those women who are going through similar situations to give themselves the permission to trust the Most High, take a deep breath and live on purpose.

No circumstance that leads you to victory is wasted. No testimony from ashes to beauty is pointless. There is something that is lies deep within each of us that was created for only for the ONE. Only one entity holds the key that unlocks the answers and peace that each of us so desires.

My prayer is that when you read my story, that you will be released from shame and guilt, true repentance is wrought, and you can find your spot among the flowers in a field of tulips.

I was sitting on my daughter's bed crying to the point of complete and total nausea. All that was going through my mind at the time was the stench of the mess I had allowed myself to get involved in. I was ashamed of ever calling myself a woman of God. I thought of my earlier years of marriage and of the fact that my husband and I actually once worked in ministry together – as a team. We had done such undeniably powerful work together and surely that was worth something. My husband came into the house and I asked him to come upstairs and just hold me. He had no idea why I was crying. There had been so many days and months and now years of off-and-on depression and bouts with anger. I asked him as he held me tight if he was praying for our marriage and he told me, "Yes, I am."

It was that small trickle of hope from his words that I assumed would be my motivation to do something about myself. However, to my surprise, I found out several days later that my husband had started divorce proceedings against me. My anger turned into fear and I spent 3 months working to convince him that I was worth him giving us another chance. Deep inside I knew my husband still loved me but he was hurt and I was the sole cause. We spent a few weeks apart and after a brush with illness, he said he no longer wanted to get the divorce and I returned home. I toiled at our relationship relentlessly. But, after a month, he was back to overworking and I found myself alone and lonely again. I didn't quite understand what it was that caused me to diligently stay committed to my duties as housewife and mother. I had a hole in my heart and neither of those responsibilities were able to heal it. I cringed at the thought of another lover, so that wasn't a solution either. I did my best to avoid any possible potential of engaging in another such situation. It was so out of my character to look for a man in the first place. They always seemed to find me, though.

Like many people do when they are not healed, I looked for what could be a positive distraction. I had been in ministry years before so I assumed returning to ministry again was my solution. Surely that would keep me occupied and on the right path. I was asked by an acquaintance to contact a family that was starting a new church in the city where I was living at the time. I thought that would be the perfect situation for me to dive into. I would attempt to make contact with the minister in the hope of arranging a meeting with him and his family and me and my family. After leaving two messages, without responses, I wasn't going to push the issue any further and resigned the idea of becoming involved in ministry altogether. Then, one day, that same minister actually returned my call. He sounded quite anointed too, I thought. I remember being introduced to him as an early adult while living in Florida. Who would have ever thought that one day we might actually be working together in ministry?

This new minister came to the church we were attending at that time and had no clue who to look for but I recognized him and went over to introduce myself. I was given the strangest stare and was not sure if he saw a demon or what, but he smiled and said it was nice to finally meet me in person. One Thursday, there was not anything particularly special about the day other than we had survived a horrible wind storm through our area, I received a call from that preacher. Something about this conversation was different. We had only had a few exchanges previously but I got that nudge in my gut that somehow I was getting close to that invisible line that screams TRESPASSING! I had not done anything wrong and once I knew he and his wife were having marital problems, I made it my business to limit my conversation with him. So why was I getting this warning? I would be lying if I said somewhere in the pit of my being I was not enjoying our conversation. After all, my husband is never around, and neither is his wife. We are only talking about ministry so what's wrong with that?

I ended that conversation only to receive a text a few hours later stating he was in the mood for giving and felt like he wanted to put some gas in my tank. Being the stupid broken woman that I was at the time, I went against everything in me and said, "Okay." We decided to meet at a gas station. So why was I putting on makeup, fixing my hair as pretty as I could get it, and finding just the right jeans, jacket and heels to put on? I told myself I was dressing modestly.

The moment I arrived at the gas station, my heart was racing. I was nervous and started to feel like I was about to sweat. He got out of his car to put the gas in my SUV and the fire that was blazing between us couldn't be quenched by all the waters of Niagara Falls. His piercing green eyes looked me up and down and he smiled and said, "You sure look nice." And like a little child, I giggled and told him, "Thanks, so do you."

Then we both avoided eye contact while we scrambled for a conversation and we ended up barely saying anything to each other. I told him, "Thank you for the gas," and he responded, "You're welcome." In my mind some words that I normally would never say came to me: "Oh shit!" It literally felt like a whirlwind had just passed through our area. Only this whirlwind was one of passion, lust, attraction, and desire for each other that had swept through that gas station and gathered us up. I got in my car, pulled out my phone to send a text message. At the same time he was sending one to me that read: "WOW!" This was the exact word I was in the process of texting.

While a new relationship was forming on one end, my husband was turning away from God on the other. After several months and to my surprise I found the divorce proceedings from my husband had been re-instated and the man I always knew as faithful, had decided to move in with another woman. I was devastated to find out that he was trying to divorce me without me knowing so he would avoid having to pay me anything. What was happening? Oh well, at least I had my preacher lover to fall back on. The preacher and I spent the next several months back and forth with our relationship until he asked me one day did I want to marry him after both of our divorces were finalized. Although I was totally in love with this man, I was dying on the inside over the breaking up of my marriage with my husband. So, of course I told him yes. He was everything I thought I wanted in a man. He was spiritual, smart, sexy, and he acted like I was the best thing since sliced bread. That's all I'd ever really wanted from my husband was to be loved and to be first in his life.

It was a never-ending whirlwind of distrust, anguish, and guilt for me with my husband. He was living with this lady who had absolutely no regards for me or his children. He and I were constantly arguing especially when my preacher lover would go into his mood swings of indecisiveness.

It was one night in March of 2009 that I experienced one of the darkest hours in my life. My husband came over to drop something off for my daughter and his countenance had turned into something I had never seen before. He looked wild and unkempt. I was feeling extremely low that night and I just wanted to talk. As usual, he had no time for me and he made it a point to be severely nasty to me. I followed him to his truck and told him I was not feeling well and asked him if he could just stay and talk to me. My husband told me there was nothing to talk about. I asked him several times in the fashion of begging and he said he didn't have anything to say to me and backed out of the driveway.

My heart ached. I felt nauseated and my head was hurting with a new level of pain. As my heart paced with intensity, I heard my children upstairs talking and playing around and I remembered that I had a bottle of pain medicine in my cabinet. I just wanted my hurt to stop. I'm not sure if dying was the goal. I just wanted quiet from my pain, my guilt, and my loneliness. As I grabbed the bottle of pills and put them to my mouth, my son walked into the kitchen and yelled, "Mom what are you doing?" I sat the pill bottle on the countertop after swallowing most of them, walked outside my back door, and lit a cigarette. It had been an easy thing to start smoking cigarettes by this time with all the drama and pain I was experiencing. I heard my son yelling saying "Oh my God, did you just take the whole bottle?" And his voice started to crack. He called my husband and asked what he had done to me to make me so upset. He told him that I'd just taken pills and that he should turn around and come back to the house. My husband told my son he was going to think about it. I heard my son tell him that if anything bad happened to me, he would kill him.

As I sat there on that back porch smoking and the noise around me begin to blur out. All I heard was the sound of inhaling and exhaling the smoke from the cigarette. I felt blank and hopeless.

"Miss Moree, can you talk to us and tell us what's going on," the gentlemen who had been called with the ambulance asked. I didn't answer him even though he asked me several times in as kind a way as he could to get me to open up. I refused to talk. I just wanted to sleep.

I have faint memories of my walking into the house and then being on a table in the ER with a belt wrapped around my body to prohibit me from leaving or moving. Two of my friends showed up completely livid with my husband. It was going to be a long night.

Needless to say my relationship with my preacher lover didn't last. His story of starting again ended in him returning to his wife and my husband cancelling the divorce and I returned back to my inner wilderness of self-hatred. I did finally get the courage to divorce my husband while I was still yet battling with the need to be saved by the touch of a man. My wilderness had gone on for 10 years now and I had had enough. It occurred to me that the only thing that would allow me to disconnect from my reality was to travel out of the country. It had been a few years since I'd travelled and to do that again meant that I had to walk away from everything: my Job, ALL Men and my Family, in an effort to save myself from destruction – at the hands of myself.

I saved up a few paychecks, renewed the passports for my daughter and myself, purchased one way plane tickets, packed up my things to leave in storage, and I left divorced, broken, bruised, guilty, angry, tired, emotional, and hurt. I was exactly where God needed me to be.

The following year I allowed myself to heal with the aid of what I call travel therapy. I got myself reacquainted with mission work and I exposed my ugly before the Lord. During my journey to rediscover who I was, I was able to totally disconnect myself from my norm. Only the mercy of God sustained me until this point. I was one hot mess!

The first thing that God made me aware of was that I had been forgiven for my past. Yes, I did reap many things in all reality but they were the consequences of my sin. However, I knew from the moment I arrived on that island that the Lord had been with me the entire time beckoning for me to return to him but I was looking for fulfillment through a person. I had listened to the myths and lies of people who told me that some men come to bring healing. That belief took away the sovereignty of the Almighty and instead caused me to idolize a man over God.

After some self-work, I finally got to the place where I believed that I was worthy of love and I was worthy of forgiveness.

The biggest challenge of all was being able to separate myself from the emotional baggage which always led me to sexual sins. I didn't need to do a forty-day fast, the Lord informed me that through my obedience, my deliverance would bring my healing. I made the commitment to be celibate. Yes, although I had shed my life of adultery; becoming a fornicator was not my goal either. I didn't want a girlfriend or a main chick status. I was brought up to believe that a wife was an honorable position; and a wife was what I wanted to be. I always knew that but I had allowed my bitterness and hurt to cause me to trade integrity for self-pleasure. And, just as the Lord had spoken, I was healed from the inside out. I had been transformed back into a woman of God and I loved me.

The most valuable lesson I have learned in all my years, is that the things we think will take years - because we try to do them within our own abilities - God can do in one day. Hence, the key is doing things His way from the start.

Meanwhile, I threw away the idea of love for a season. Not that I didn't want it, but I was no longer going to compromise my integrity for anybody and I was no longer going to be led by my emotions. I spent years wrestling back and forth with the darkness and despair over my life and I was not willing to trade my peace for anybody or anything. I recall hearing people say that God had a sense of humor. I found that to be so true when my life turned around and I remarried my husband that I once thought I hated so much. Yeah, God does have a sense of humor!

Penetrating Innocence

By: C. J. Lane

C.J. Lane

AUTHOR OF:

CONFESSIONS OF THE OTHER WOMAN

TALES OF AN UNDISCOVERED WRITER

cj@cjLane.me

www.cjlane.me

To the Powerful Person reading this:

I didn't start with this story. I wrote another story that I was going to submit for this book. It was only telling half of my story though. It was showing my life with issues but in a pretty package. It wasn't the nasty gritty truth of what happen to me. I was trying to cheat the process but I should have known that I couldn't do that. I realized that I was still embarrassed by it not to mention it is still a secret. It is an unfortunately usual act done in an unusual way. I was sure that the moment someone read my words surely my skin was going to burn off of my body. Then I realized that I wasn't just writing this story for myself. I was writing this story for you, the person reading this. Whether you are a woman going through your own pain or a man or woman trying to understand how a woman processes pain, what it looks like, and what might cause it. Whatever your reason for reading this I hope that this story speaks to you and heals you as much as it has healed me writing it.

This story was very difficult to share. But I know it was necessary for my healing and growth. It has a greater purpose however and that is to heal the masses. I had to get over the fact that after this story when people see me they would probably see the act that was performed on me or me as damaged goods. I felt lost coming through my Exodus until I read I Know Why the Caged Bird Sings by Maya Angelou. When I read her experience and how she overcame it strengthened me, gave me hope, and help me get through. I hope that my story does the same for you. I hope that you see how I survived my pain and know that you can do the same. I spill my blood through my pen for you because I am my sister's keeper.

Yours Truly,
C. J. Lane

I took a bath the night before and that was the last time I felt clean. I noticed that the bathroom was smaller to me than I remembered. I guess that should have been a sign. All of a sudden I could hardly move through the little room. It was like I was inside of a dollhouse. I chuckled at the thought, "Me inside of a dollhouse? Yeah right!" I didn't like dolls let alone the "houses" they supposedly lived in. I could never understand why girls wasted their time with them. I looked in the mirror. I had grown, gotten taller, and filled out just as a sixteen-year-old should. The problem was that I was eleven. My D-cup bra served as proof that I was blessed with ample curves to share. Boys were starting to notice my shape. I knew this because their eyes wandered and lingered on certain places. Their gazes held something different when they looked at me that wasn't there before.

I shook my head and turned my focus back to the room. It looked like the inside of a Pepto Bismol bottle - pink curtains, pink rugs, and pink walls. I mean even the toilet seat was pink! My aunt was girly and her two daughters followed right behind her with petticoat dresses, Barbie dolls, and curls. As you could probably tell I was not girly, no scratch that, I was anti-girly! I couldn't stand dresses and I hated the color pink! That's why my changing relationships with my male friends upset me. It wasn't that I didn't like being a girl, I just didn't like girly things. I didn't like the invisible rules or the separation that was taking place. Boys and I used to climb trees together. Now, they're falling out of them because they are too busy looking at me. Women were always telling me to stop climbing trees, stop being so rough, and stop acting like a boy. But that is just it, I didn't act like a boy, I was just being myself. As I looked behind the door to see what my aunt had left me to sleep in, I noticed that it was pink with ruffles on the collar. I sighed and then I put on my aunt's pretty pink nightgown.

The next morning I woke up excited because it was a Saturday. After my stressful week dealing with school work, friends, bullies and my parents' divorce, my plan was to sit around all day in my PJ's watching cartoons. You know, we never know when our last moment of childhood will be. It comes out of nowhere like a flash. It's interesting how things change in a matter of moments, seconds, minutes, or hours. Things that slowly deprived a childhood of the love and nourishment that it needs until there is nothing left but a shell that blows away in the wind. It never occurred to me that losing innocence comes with a cost. I couldn't have guessed that mine would start that day.

My uncle sat relaxed with his elbows resting on the dining room table. He and my aunt weren't married, but he had been there since I could remember so he had earned the title, "uncle." I smiled at him like he smiled at us when he chased us around the house making us giggle. I loved when he played music and we danced around the apartment. The smell of his morning drink of gin and juice attacked my nose and made me wrinkle up my face. It was usually an indication of...nothing. That is just it, I don't remember him not drinking. It was normal. I don't remember him being an angry drunk, but I do remember his face from time to time being frowned up like he was really upset about something. Not today though he smiled at me and I reciprocated. Galloping feet grabbed my attention as I slid under the table just in time for the younger children to run past.

I was laying there watching TV when by some change in the current of neurons in my "uncle's" brain made him decide to take his foot and put it under my gown. At first, I thought it was an accident. I didn't pay it any mind the first two times. I thought that maybe his foot had slipped. Then, I realized what was happening. I felt my blood churn as his callused, roughened skin rubbed up my leg, longer and further each time. I scooted away on the soft, beige carpet as my mind went through the denial that maybe I was in his way. That was until the further away I moved, the closer he got. He leaned back in his yellow chair and rolled it across the floor inching closer to me. It was silent as it glided across the fibers like an animal stalking its prey. If I could hear it maybe it would be a warning, a branch snapping under one's foot alerting the pack, but there was no warning. When I couldn't move over anymore, my legs were forced open by his lower extremities. My heart stopped as he entered me. The round firmness of his big toe expanded my young virgin walls. My heart hardened as he moved it in and out. My will was weakened and I was frozen in fear of what I am not sure. The shame and embarrassment that I felt lengthened the time and turned minutes into hours. Then five seconds after forever, it finally stopped. The whole time I laid there screaming inside hoping that someone would come and rescue me, remove me from this impossible situation. This impossible but happening situation. How was this happening? Maybe it wasn't happening...maybe it was in my head? Maybe that's why no one came? If only I could close my eyes and he would be gone. I closed my eyes but he was still there torturing me. The horrible feeling that was happening in my chest was still there. My heart was racing. I was mad that I was being violated, sad that it was someone I loved, and confused about why it was happening to me.

I told my mother as soon as I saw her. My mom is the strongest, bravest, and smartest person I know. So I figured she would know what to do. She sat there while I told her looking out of the window. The more I spoke the more her face contorted and tears welled up in her eyes. Her hands, once resting calmly on the steering wheel were now balled up tiny fists gripping the wheel. I knew that she was hurt for me and that she was ready to go off on someone for her child! And she did. I just didn't expect that person to be me. I was the person bombarded with questions that I just could not answer, "Why didn't you run and scream? Why didn't you tell your aunt? Why did you let him do that to you? What did you do?" I was told that there was going to be a talk with my aunt and I was to wait.

I thought up so many different outcomes to this problem that I had now caused. I thought that he would try to kill my mom or my aunt. That he would try to do this to another girl or even worst he would try to do it again to me. After about a month of constant nightmares, I went to my mom worried asking what was going to be done. She sighed and went on to explain to me that the daughters that he produced should not be subjected to the embarrassment and ridicule of having a father that raped his niece with his big toe. So I broke down, "What about me," I thought. "What about my embarrassment?" I didn't understand. I was so confused. Tears ran down my face and I almost fell to my knees. I wanted to scream! "Why was all of this happening to me? Wasn't I too a child?" Any ideas that I had that my age would matter were thrown out the window, ran over by a truck, and tossed in the gutter when my mother said, "What happen to you wasn't nothing! I've had a lot worse happen to me. So suck it up and stop acting like a baby!" So I shut up and I shut down.

Even four years later, when I sat in front of what would be my first of many mental health therapists, I couldn't bring anything up about it because I was warned that it was a private matter. That no one needed to know. Even when I could talk about it, I wouldn't deal with it. I thought that talking about the rape without really talking about how it related to me was enough.

How my mother dealt with the situation and the fact that this was done to me by someone who I considered family set the standard. If I wasn't safe at home, then where was I safe? If my mother couldn't be bothered to protect me, then who? After that everything else was common practice like being used and abused by people in my life.

I become the statistic that everyone spoke about. I was fulfilling a prophecy put on me the very moment that my "uncle's" skin touched mine. I was so hurt and confused by what happened to me, I felt unattractive. So when boys approached me about sex, I was thrown so off guard that they even wanted to do something like that with me that I quickly did what they wanted before they changed their minds. I did whatever I could to make them happy because I thought that would in turn make me happy.

Six years after it was stolen from me, a poor, ignorant, misguided, girl on a dining room floor, I gave it away. Something I didn't have. The first time that a man entered my body, something very important to me was taken away too soon. The next time that a man entered my body, something important was given to me too early, and it changed my life forever. Seven months after I gave myself to a man, my son entered this world. The only reason that I hadn't had sex up until that point was because I was trying to be good. In the end, I got tired of having my virginity. This thing that was supposed to make me pure when I already felt so dirty. Maybe I thought that it was a lie that I didn't want to live anymore.

For years I went around trying to collect as much love as I could from men. As hard as I would try, I couldn't get full because I didn't know that to fill something you have to fix the holes. There was a big gaping hole in the bottom of my heart; whatever I put in came right back out in the form of anxiety and self-loathing. My idea of love was warped. I didn't quite know what I was looking for but I knew it was something I didn't have.

I just knew that there was something wrong with me. I was tainted and if people realized how much, they would never want anything to do with me. I didn't see my love as anything worthy. So I wouldn't charge much for it. For a smile, a kiss or a kind word, I would give everything I could in thanks for showing me attention no matter how slight. Being hungry for attention is like a neon light to soul vultures. People who prey on the souls of others to feed themselves. They follow you around waiting for the perfect time to strike. When you are at your most vulnerable point. They slide in and rob you of your heart.

There was the guy who loved me so much that he threw knives at me. He threatened to kill himself for me. I promised that I would love him through whatever. That was the worst mistake I ever made in my life. He had me hiding knives under my pillow in order to sleep in case I needed to protect myself. He used fear to keep me near him. Fear of him hurting me, fear of him hurting himself, fear of me going back on my word, and fear of me being alone.

There was another man who played on my emotions. He used his voice and charm to get into my heart and his award-winning acting to chain me blindly to him. He, who wasn't even with me at the time, made me promise to give myself to only him. When I slept with someone else he cried real tears because he was so hurt. I cried with him. I felt lower than low so I was placed in the make-up zone. I was so busy making it up to him that I almost missed the fact that he was using me to cheat on his wife that I didn't know he had.

By the time that I reached my late twenties, I had been so conditioned to receive and accept madness that I married someone I never should have. I used the equation: years known divided by the years we had sex to stand in the place of a relationship that never really existed. He was my go-to back scratcher when I had an itch, and I was his go-to honey pot when he needed something sweet. We were always there when neither of us were taken to fill in. There was never a relationship, but I had to make it sound official. I couldn't tell people that we got together in April and married in November because it would sound as unreal as it was. We didn't go on a date for the first seven years of this so-called relationship, we just had sex and he was cool with that until he needed a place to stay. I then took a very thin layer of forged politeness to make me see the good in someone. He knew when to say please and thank you, but was rarely pleased and never meant thanks. Also, a thin layer of commonality for me to run off to the alter. Truth is, we didn't have much in common so the things we did I held on to like the rare gems they were. I told myself that we were meant to be when the truth is that I never believed that there was going to be anyone else. I thought that this person was the best I was going to get so I had better not miss my chance. I knew the day after my wedding that I had made a great mistake, but it was too late. I had taken vows before God and I had to try as hard as I could to make it work. Four months later after the cheating, the screaming, the lies, and the abuse I decided that it wasn't going to work for me or my son.

After I ended my marriage, I decided to let go and let God. I was tired of dealing with men who not only weren't for me, they were detrimental to my health. I said a prayer that God would send the man who I was meant to be with to me. I prayed that God would help me know and understand my worthiness. That I would have the patience to wait for him and the eyes to see him when he showed up.

On July 17th, 2014, three months after my divorce, I started talking to the man of my dreams. We got married on December 13th, 2014. The experience has been a great one and God has shown me through this man what true human love is.

I am mending my holes which started with forgiveness for all parties involved, including myself. My mother and I had a very tumultuous relationship after the incident. We were pretty much at each other's throats all of my teenaged years. I could not see how she could put his girls over me. I resented her for it. It seemed to me that every time I tried to heal the opportunity was taking away from me. She would say things like I wasn't raped because he didn't use his penis. Every time I said the word rape, she would say molested. It wasn't until I was old enough to look up the word myself that I knew the truth and could stand on it. "Rape," unlawful sexual intercourse or any other sexual penetration of the vagina, anus or mouth of another person with or without force by a sex organ, other body part or foreign object without the consent of the victim. After I became mature enough to know the real meaning of and the meaning behind words, I was able to finally figure out the words my mother said. What she said was, "What happen to you wasn't nothing! I've had a lot worse happen to me. So suck it up and stop acting like a baby!" What she meant, "In my mind, what I went through was much worse than what you went through and no one did anything for me so I don't really know the right thing to do for you, but I'm fine and you will be too." Once I saw her words this way I was able to forgive my mom, she was playing with the cards she had been dealt. Sure she could have played them in a different order, but once a card is played that's it.

Recently my mother and I had a talk where she admitted everything that happened to me. She told me that the real reason she didn't file charges is because she didn't want me to have to relive the event over and over again. She didn't want it to be his word against mine. I was shocked, but because I had already forgiven her, I was able to hear and accept what she had to say. She didn't know that I had relived the event every time that I had a nightmare and woke up in a cold sweat wondering if he was hiding in my room. I didn't have a scary, hairy monster hiding in my room, it was him behind the door and under the bed.

My rapist has since passed away but before he died, I hadn't seen him for years. While he was on his deathbed, I kept getting requests from his daughter to pray for him. She still doesn't know what happen between us. I take praying seriously so I wanted to pray for him but I had so many reasons not too. I talked with God. I prayed for him to give me the strength and I remembered something my mother told me, "You don't forgive people for them, you forgive people for yourself. They will still live their life or afterlife while you are still left carrying the burden they left on you." I realized that I was tired of carrying this burden. I also knew that God will deal with this man the way he saw fit if he hadn't done so already. So before he passed, I prayed for him and his soul to find peace.

I am still working on myself which I have found is the hardest part. Instead of cleaning and removing the cesspool of this incident, I have built layers up over the years. I thought it would hide the stench, cover up the scars and mask the embarrassment. I've learned that layers are a temporary fix, a band aid. Eventually, the smell comes through, cuts get deeper, and the mask fades away. After all of that layering, you still need to fix the problem - the rotting, infected gash underneath. Now, because of the lack of care, there has to be a careful breakdown and reconstruction to repair the injury that penetrated my innocence. After years of dealing with this pain, embarrassment, and low self-esteem, I realized that even though others may have dropped the ball in my life it was up to me to pick it up again. Not only have I picked up the ball I am playing with it. I am doing spectacular things to uplift myself. I have created a loving family with my son and husband. I am helping others by releasing my pain through my pen and writing this story. I am doing all I can to help myself and others. After all, I'm not a child anymore...

My David and Goliath Story

By: Carol Evans Ryan

Carol Evans Ryan
carol.ryan01@gmail.com

Dear Reader,

I am so glad to be able to give you a glimpse into my life. This has been the most amazing journey, just like a well-planned and constructed rollercoaster. I have had to patiently make the slow climb up the hill to experience the exhilaration of the great plunge off the top peak. At times the ride is scary. At other times it is something I choose to experience again and again for the sheer fun of it all!"

No matter where you are on this path of brokenness and healing, it is my hope that you find something in my story that you can embrace as part of your own. I hope you find some helpful stones to put into your slingshot. I invite you to come alongside me and let our paths intertwine. As we mingle together, I will contribute something to your life and you will contribute something to mine. I would love to hear your story, to bear witness to your pain and to your healing.

I invite you to borrow some of my hope today if you can't seem to find some of your own. But if you persevere, if you stubbornly push through, you will find your own hope. If you keep pushing past the suffering, not only will you find hope, but you will find joy. And one day, you will share your hope with someone else who has lost theirs.

I pray that my story offers you courage and hope. My favorite Bible verse is Jeremiah 29:11.

> "For I know the thoughts that I think toward you, saith the LORD, thoughts of peace, and not of evil, to give you an expected end."

An expected end. An architect designs a building that initially doesn't appear to be much more than blue lines drawn on newsprint using a ruler. But the architect knows that one day it will be an amazing structure, built to house beautiful art work.

It doesn't matter what someone else intended for you. God, your very own architect, has a plan for you. An expected end. He thinks good thoughts about you. He smiles when He thinks of you. His heart beats faster with joy over you.

He has plans of peace. He has a plan for you, just as He did for me. It's not the plan I thought it would be, but my life is far, far better than anything I had ever imagined. I encourage you to believe in the loving plan God has for you. Reach out and grab it! Take my hand and walk this journey with me and allow me to walk your journey with you. You may write and tell me your story; what you've endured deserves a witness, and as a fellow survivor, I'd be honored to walk that path with you. I'm just a stone, but am mighty in the Father's hands.

Nathan, one of my little buddies from long ago called my hugs "squeeze hugs." Today, I am sending both gentle and squeeze hugs for you.

From one living, breathing stone to another, Carol

I was raised in the Deep South. I grew up in Savannah, Georgia, surrounded by an Irish-American family and a community rich in history, steeped in southern charm and tradition. At first glance, the scene appears picturesque. : However, as a little girl, I experienced a broken family: parents marrying, divorcing, and remarrying, and continually gaining and losing half- and step-brothers and sisters. There was a lot of turmoil and change.

When I was three years-old, my stepfather began sexually abusing me. He was particularly fond of torture and delighted in the pain of others. Shortly into their marriage, he began abusing my mother as well. Many nights I lay awake, terrified that either my mother or I would be dead in the morning. I felt invisible to the world, but somehow could not escape the eyes of the predator living in our home.

As a young child, I took great comfort in my relationship with Jesus Christ. I read the Bible often and particularly loved the stories of the Old Testament. One story stood out vividly in my mind's eye. It was the story of David and Goliath, as told in I Samuel 17. This is a paraphrase of the story.

> The Israelite army was doing battle against the terrifying Philistine army. One of the Philistine soldiers was particularly

menacing. Goliath, a giant who was more than nine feet tall - a decorated warrior dressed in the best armor - carried a big spear. He was arrogant and bold. Every morning and every night for forty days, he would shout insults at the Israelites and their God.

He challenged the men of the Israelite army. "No one can defeat me! Not even your God can defeat me! You and your God are afraid of me. I challenge you! If one of you will come out and fight me and win, we will submit and become your servants. But if I win, you will become our servants."

This made the Israelites very angry. Yet they remained still. They hoped and prayed that someone, anyone, would come forward and fight this horrible giant, but not one of them volunteered to do the job. They didn't think they could win that battle.

A young shepherd boy named David was visiting his older brothers in the camp and heard this arrogant giant shouting his taunts at the Israelites. David was shocked and angry. "How dare this ungodly man swear at the Israelite army and say horrible things about our God!"

David asked, "Isn't anyone going to do something about this? Isn't anyone here brave enough to go out and fight this man?" All the other Israelites took a figurative step backward and it became apparent that David alone was the only one willing to fight this giant and defend God's honor.

The Israelite king, Saul, was so happy that someone, even if that someone was a child, was willing to fight Goliath. I can only imagine how terrified they had to be to allow a small child - someone trained to tend sheep and not trained as a soldier - to go out and represent them on the battlefield knowing that if David lost the battle, they would all become slaves to the Philistines. King Saul had his men put his very own armor on David. They handed him Saul's spear and pushed him toward the enemy's line. David, feeling awkward and clumsy in Saul's oversized armor, knew he could not do battle this way. The very armor designed to protect the king during battle would cause him to stumble when he walked, much less fought. David, believing that God was more than capable of winning this battle, took off the clumsy armor.

Then he chose five small stones and, in true little boy courage, stepped forward to do battle with Goliath, wearing nothing more than his shepherd's smock and carrying his trusty slingshot. As he stepped forward, he said, "I will fight this man and God will win!" Goliath laughed. He was angered that a mere child was sent to do battle. Not willing to back down, though, he decided this fight would be entertaining to the troops. He stepped forward, ready to squash this child who was not even half his height.

David loaded one stone into his slingshot. He pulled back the leather strap, aimed, and fired one shot. One small pebble penetrated a tiny hole in Goliath's armor. When that pebble hit Goliath's forehead, Goliath fell down dead. David proclaimed the victory was God's. The armies were more than stunned. This kid had just killed the fiercest warrior in the land! No one saw that coming!

I took great comfort in this story. God could help a little kid win, even when the enemy was nine feet tall!

The Goliath in my life is a psychiatrist's laundry list of symptoms one would hope to not see in one's patient. However, the reality is that my Goliath is actually a history of prolonged, sustained child abuse that began at the age of three and spanned the remainder of my childhood and young adulthood. I always thought that my stepfather was Goliath. I'd read in the book of Psalms and hear David begging for God's mercy and protection. I knew exactly how he was feeling; running, hiding, gathering supplies. It wasn't until later that I began to understand my Goliath was the effects of the abuse, not the abuser himself.

For years I only understood the fear, intimidation, and lies. I instinctively knew the tools at my disposal: being invisible, being as perfect as possible, constantly staying on hyper alert status, anticipating the enemy's next move, being aware of the emotional atmosphere of everyone in the room, and doing whatever it took to keep everyone happy or at least calm, unaware, and distracted. I did not understand the true nature of the evil inflicted on this small child. Ideas contrary to what I'd grown up with were completely foreign to me. I never knew there was such a thing as personal boundaries or better yet that I should and could have my own personal boundaries. I thought that if anyone knew the thoughts in my head, I'd be taken away by the men in white coats to a place for the mentally unstable, a place resembling a cemetery more than a hospital. A place where I'd be locked up, alone and forgotten forever.

Just as David appeared to be too small for the task of saving Israel from the Philistines, I appeared to be too small to escape my inner turmoil, the dark sensations of hell that were my constant companions. Just as Saul tried to outfit David in his own over-sized armor, I tried to mold armor out of forgetfulness and denial. My movements were as clumsy as David in Saul's armor. Personal relationships suffered. Teachers stared, completely dumbfounded by the discrepancy of my abilities, one day working at a very high level in gifted classes and the next day appearing to be quite deficient and belonging in remedial classes. Family members simply looked the other way, hoping the Philistines would bore with the incredibly unbalanced fight and walk away. My subconscious dealt with all of this in a series of strange yet creative methods, unaware to my conscious mind.

I knew I wasn't like other children. I knew because Marcia, Jan, and Cindy Brady didn't live like this. Opie Taylor never feared his father. The Beaver was always happy and carefree. All the other children at school seemed to enjoy life and not have a care in the world.

I thought that was normal and I so badly craved that normalcy. I wanted someone to tousle my hair and smile, not ram me against the wall or choke me until I passed out. I desperately desired for my mother and father to tuck me in bed, covers pulled up to my chin, and for the covers to still be in place in the morning. I wanted for my mother and father to wake me cheerfully in the morning, for the sunshine to be the only visitor in my bedroom until then.

It wasn't until I went to Southeastern Bible College, now Southeastern University, that I began to understand true normalcy was somewhere in between my Hollywood influenced fantasy world and the horror of my childhood. At the age of 17, I moved away from home for the first time and began to see what was normal. God incredibly and mercifully brought Doug and Rosemary Bailey into my life. This family lived only a block away from the college. Through a series of God-orchestrated events, I lived with the Baileys when campus housing was closed. The Baileys were a loving and caring family, but I had only seen them in good times. I was sure that there was more to this story.

I vividly recall the first disagreement I witnessed Doug and Rosemary having. My stomach tightened into a knot and my focus became blurry as I prepared for one of them to begin beating the other one. That is all I had known in my childhood and that was normal in my mind. I waited for the sound of flesh hitting flesh, the sound of a woman crying and pleading for mercy, but those sounds did not begin.

Instead, I heard Doug and Rosemary disagree in

calm, confident voices. They both felt strongly about what they were discussing and that it was clear they had opposite viewpoints. However, they spoke politely and were respectful of each other. No one scattered. Their small children continued to play happily in the living room. No voices were raised.

The discussion weighed the pros and cons of the choice at hand. They each decided to go about their day and mull over the conversation, giving adequate space and time for each to reconsider their position. Later, Doug and Rosemary came back together and shared their opinions. They were both still in the same mindset they had been in earlier; neither had changed their opinion. I remained frozen in my invisible state of being, waiting for the real fight to begin. Instead, the atmosphere was calm, peaceful, and loving.

Then I heard these words, "Well, I still feel like I did before, but if it really means that much to you, then I'm okay with it." There was a kiss, a hug, and a smile. Then dinner was on the table. No furniture was broken. No one was bloodied. No slamming doors. No driving off angrily down the street. Just dinner on the table; love and caring all around. That was the day I began to thaw. That was the day that I witnessed what real love is and how a Godly marriage works.

That was the beginning of God whispering to me about the possibilities of life. My future started to become brighter; a soft light at first. He began showing me stones to choose from. He told me to put down the spear of fear, anger, and denial. He began showing me smaller, more perfect stones such as counseling, talking, admitting that it happened, and sharing with other people. There were many choices of stones. Some were therapy, medication, cognitive and behavioral changes, but best of all, truth and love.

Once I had the slingshot and had chosen the stones, just as David had, I stepped out to fling the stones at my real Goliath. Sometimes I fling the stones bravely, recognizing that God is the One Who is doing the directing, hitting the mark perfectly. At other times I wobble a bit here and there, letting the taunts of the Philistines enter my ears, pervading my thoughts. But then God says to draw back the leather strap of the sling of love and therapy and then, "Boom!" It hits the target dead on.

I wish I could say that I was always confident, but I can't. However, I can confidently say that God is leading me out of this, even though it is taking more than a few stones, more than one aim, more than one shot.

I have since learned that I am not alone. I am not

the only one by far. I think back to my third grade classroom and it saddens me that there were most likely others living in a hell of their very own to which I was oblivious. It is generally accepted that one in four girls and one in eight boys have experienced the same terror of childhood sexual abuse. I have learned that I can change my future and allow God to use my experiences to help and encourage others, much like we are encouraged and emboldened by David's story in the Bible.

Two of the precious stones God pointed out to me were Doug and Rosemary Bailey. I owe so much to them and their family. Graciously, their daughters Sherri, Laurie, Susan, and Kate shared their parents and their home with me, even though I was just a broken girl. Through the love of this family and God's faithfulness, I became less and less broken. I learned so much in their home, from how to bake an apple pie to how to be a loving wife and mother.

Before the Bailey's entered my life, God sent other precious stones to me. Men and women in my home church who loved on me and helped me grow in my faith. Teachers who invested time and effort into my life, above and beyond the call of their profession. A Girl Scout troop leader who taught me about love while teaching me how to build an effective campfire. After the Bailey's entered my life, God sent even more precious stones. These were professors, counselors, and friends. All of these stones were flawed, yet godly men and women willing to be used by God in my life. There are so many - too many, in fact, to name.

Each one brought a special and wonderful gift to the table. They would enter my life by means of what appeared to be insignificant coincidences, but were in reality, divine intervention. They would walk away after having made a huge impact on my life and leaving a small piece of armor for which to cloak myself in. I'd put on one piece of armor at a time: the piece of armor of understanding that I could safely take an anti-depressant to combat chemical changes in my brain due to depression; the piece that taught me I could be flawed and still loveable; the piece that said through hard work, perseverance, and courage, I could allow a mental health counselor to walk by my side for several years as a witness to my pain and my growth; a piece that said there is still hope and life is worth living; the piece that said I still had something beautiful to bring into the lives of many other people.

At age 23, I married Mark, the love of my life. He is a gem above all gems. He deserves so much more than I can ever give him in this lifetime. Together, we have a beautiful family of our own. Our adult daughters, Sarah and Katie are creative, talented, strong, loving, and kind. They were and are amazing, but they had to go through their own growing pains to become the awesome women they are. I am so proud to be their mother.

This doesn't mean our family was perfect. No, this is not a fairy tale; we were and are a normal family. Mark and I had to learn to grow together, to be strong together, to be weak together, and to become a single vessel made of two flawed beings. We had to learn to be flexible and allow God to make us into what He could use in other people's lives. Simple stones. That's who we are.

After homeschooling our children for ten years, I returned to school and earned my Bachelor's Degree in Practical Theology 29 years after I began that educational pursuit. With that momentum, I pressed on and earned my Master's Degree in Professional Counseling. I always thought I'd grow up to be a missionary one day. You know what? I did. I just didn't understand what my mission field would look like. The picture is so much more than I had ever imagined. My life is full. My life is complete.

We bought that little house from Doug and Rosemary Bailey. I had lived there off and on while in college, and then later Mark lived there, too. It's where I learned to love. In that dining room is where Mark presented me with my engagement ring. In that side yard, we sat on the swing and shared our first kiss after he proposed.

By the driveway was the light pole I backed Mark up against when we had our first argument. It was the same driveway where we eventually taught each of our little girls how to ride a bicycle. It was the same kitchen where they learned how to make a pie. It was the same home where they learned how to have an argument with - and still respect - their partners .It's that precious home where our daughters were raised by flawed, human parents; that same home where love continued to flow. That house was and is a testament to all that God has done in our lives.

Currently, I am working in the field of mental health counseling and am able to be empathetic and offer unconditional positive regard to my clients, coworkers, and friends, just as others have offered me over the years. I am blessed to be the stone that God has chosen to use in other women's lives. I've had the privilege of working with women who are convicted felons and addicted to drugs; people dealing with severe and persistent mental disorders such as Depression, Schizophrenia, Bipolar Disorder, and Post-Traumatic Stress Disorder; family members experiencing domestic violence; sexual assault victims in the first hours after the assault; and the homeless population, helping them find food, shelter, and mental health care when needed.

It is an honor to go into psychiatric units, to be alongside persons who, just days before, saw no hope in life and contemplated and/or attempted suicide. I know that despair and blessedly, I now have enough hope to share with my clients. That's how I got through some of the darkest days of my life. I would show up in my counselor's office feeling no hope. He would tell me, "I have so much hope for you, plenty enough to spare. Why don't you borrow some of mine today until you find some of your own?" He assured me that I would find some of my own. And he was right.

As a mental health counselor, some days are delightful, such as when a clean and sober mother is reunited with her children. Other days are heart wrenching and difficult, such as the day I learned one of my "Bridge" girls died from a heroin overdose. All days are blessed, as I am privileged to offer the kindness and love to others that were offered so often to me.

I learned that through God's love that broken girls and boys can grow up to become strong warriors, defeating the many Goliaths that were placed in our paths to disable us. Healing is not an easy path. It requires a lot of patience and acceptance. I had to learn to embrace acceptance. I used to interpret acceptance as a passive word. It's not. I mistakenly thought it meant that I accepted and condoned the evil that was perpetrated on me as a child. It doesn't.

I didn't want my past to include such horrible pain, but the fact is that it does. I didn't want to have to take an anti-depressant, but I did. I didn't want healing to take years of therapy, but it did. I didn't want to let my emotions out and cry all those tears, but I did. I had to do the hard work. We all have to do the hard work to get where we want to be. We can't just click our heels together and arrive at wholeness, happiness, and contentment; however, we can all get there. We can walk this journey together.

There are many of us out there, at varying stages of healing. We can reach out and receive help from someone else along the way. Thankfully, we can also offer help to others along the way. As we enter each other's lives, we each grow and benefit from the relationship, whether we are on the strong end or the weak end of the struggle. I have witnessed many times the fact that God never does just one thing at a time.

While He is allowing me to help strengthen and heal you, He is allowing you to help strengthen and heal me. No matter how broken we are we always have something to give to another person, be it perspective, strength, courage, wisdom, or friendship. One of the sayings in Narcotics Anonymous is, "We can only keep what we have by giving it away." By sharing our hope with others, we grow our own hope. By sharing our recovery, we grow our own recovery. My personal experiences have taught me the truth of this saying.

I am, along with many of you, victorious and so incredibly thankful and grateful. God is merciful. He is loving. His mercy endures forever. Amen.

Openly Broken

By: Candace Smith

Candace L. Smith

Openly.broken@gmail.com
Openlybroken2015.blogspot.com

Dear Reader,

I decided to write this short recount of a very personal, sad, and embarrassing moment in my life for two reasons: to help myself and to possible help someone else. Because of this decision I've learned a few things along the way. First, depression is very real. Secondly, depression amongst African American men and women does not nearly get the recognition it deserves. According to an article written by Nia Hamm, "Black women are among the most undertreated groups for depression in the nation, which can have serious consequences for the African-American community."

I hope to accomplish a couple of things by writing this. First, I hope to start a very uncomfortable but needed conversation on the subject. Secondly, I hope to learn more and then share more on the subject because knowledge is indeed power.

I want you the reader to know that I struggled with the

ending of this story. I read it over and over again and I cringe because I don't want for anyone to finish it and think, "Aww she found her happy ending." This is absolutely not true. It was the beginning to seeing a possible happy ending if that makes any sense. I still struggle everyday with depression, (even writing that sentence took great effort.) Nevertheless, moving forward is my only option so here I am looking for answers that I've asked of myself for years without ever expecting any real answers.

This is where you come in. If you're looking for a confidential place to help me start this conversation or share your own personal stories please feel free to contact me with the information listed above.

C. Smith

I am a black woman.
I am strong.
Regal.
Always confident.

It took me almost thirty minutes to find the place. I almost gave up a dozen or so times. The voice in my mind kept telling me to just turn around. This was a waste of time. But I kept moving forward. When I arrived I sat in the parking lot and cried. It was such a beautiful day. I could be doing almost anything else but this. I could be almost anywhere else but here. But that was the problem. Lately I couldn't do anything. The effort it took to pull the covers off of me in the morning was exhausting. When the sun peaked through my curtains in the morning I wanted the day to be over. I remembered when the start of a new day was just that, a brand new start, a new beginning. It's amazing how things can change so drastically. Inside I wanted to just leave; however, I knew that I needed this. I craved the day that a new day would be just that, new.

I am a black woman.
I am strong.
I have soft hard-working hands that can do almost anything.
I have a sharp mind.

I was over an hour early. I don't know why but I felt like I needed time to prepare myself. I needed to prepare to finally be honest. I needed to prepare myself not to smile and appear to be happy. I realized that I'd had my whole life to practice how to smile when I wanted to cry, laugh when I wanted to scream, and just cover up my true feelings. I realized that the face I showed the world and even myself was a facade, an imitation of what I wished I was. I cried harder. I cried a cry whose birth place was the most inner pit of my stomach and upon reaching maturity, it had gained the strength it needed to claw its way through my intestines, up past my heart seeming to choke the very life out of me. As it crawled over my vocal chords, masterminding a manipulative escape to its own freedom route, that seemed to break through my teeth, much like a baby alligator breaks through the white egg shell holding it hostage from taking its first breath.

> ***I am a black woman.***
> ***I am strong.***
> ***I am strong with or without.***
> ***I look my strongest when I am alone.***

A grey car pulled in and a casually dressed woman got out of the car. She walked confidently with a relaxed stride to a set of uniformed office doors differing only by the large wooden numbers nailed in the center. Her door was labeled, number one, with a small ornament hanging from a hook that I couldn't quite see from where I was parked. I was instantly jealous. She probably didn't have a care in the world. She woke every morning to her perfect house, husband and kids, and drove leisurely to her perfect job. Her biggest concern was probably traffic and if the weather would ruin little Timmy's softball game on Saturday. What could she do for me?

I am a black woman.
I am strong.
But I am alone.

I waited for a few minutes after she went into the building to finally wipe the remaining tears off of my face. I checked my hair and make-up in the mirror. I sprayed on a few pumps of my perfume, slipped out of my flats into my heels, and got out of the car. The walk to her office from car seemed so long. My feet felt very heavy and every step took so much effort. I had to think about every step. I ignored the shouts in my head to retreat. By the time I reached the door I had sweated through my favorite suit and blouse combo. I knocked because I didn't know rather I could just enter. I didn't hear anything but I waited. A few moments later the door opened and I was greeted with the warmest smile and sincerest eyes.

I followed her into a small office where she allowed me to choose where I would be most comfortable to sit. She sat directly across from me. I realized that the whole entire room was set up that way. No matter where I sat she would always be directly in front of me.

I was glad the place had a homey feel. There were pictures on the wall that represented something from just about every religion or culture. I guess she wanted whoever came here to feel comfortable and represented. The array of religious items made me more uncomfortable because it told me nothing about her.

I am a black woman.
I am strong.
Always knowing what to say.
I have an understanding ear.

I was glad she was a she. I was glad she was white. I don't think I could have sat before a black woman preparing myself to tell her how weak I am. How I'm not strong enough these days to keep it together. A white woman would be more understanding to this. I thought.

A moment or two after I had sat a rush of emotion engulfed me. How did I get here? Why am I here? I don't belong here.

My palms began to sweat. I had to take several deep breaths.

We sat staring at each other for a moment or two too long for my taste. She smiling. Me fighting the urge not to smile back as to not appear to be okay and the urge to burst into tears all at the same time. It was like going to the doctor's office after feeling sick for days only to get there and feel better and have to sort of pretend to be sicker than you actually felt at the moment. Or taking your car to the mechanic only for your car to suddenly stop making the noise it had been making for over a month. It drives you kind of crazy. All of a sudden I felt ridiculous. I felt better. Like talking about me was a waste of time. Maybe it was just a fluke. Maybe I just needed to pray harder, fast longer, or read more of my Bible. This was just a test. Should I make more of an effort to be to church on time? Should I stay for all three services instead of two? Should I try to make it to early Morning Prayer? Maybe I was listening to too much secular music.

"So, how are you feeling today," she calmly asked slowly enunciating each word.

My eyes immediately filled with tears. I hate it when people ask me questions like that. It made me realize that even on my happiest day there is always something wrong. Some unspoken, unrealized sadness that sits in the corner of my mind that I have chosen (for that day) not to give my full attention too. This at least allows me a temporary relief. Or was it that finally someone had asked me, (the strong, independent, I can do it all by myself I don't need anyone's help, as long as I got King Jesus I'm okay), how am I feeling. I figured that people don't usually ask that question unless they had a motive, angle, or just nosy. My daddy (God rest his soul) always told me, "no one is going to give you anything for free. Everything comes with a price." Rarely had I found this not to be true. But this was one of those rare moments. Now all I had to do was find the strength to finally be honest. This simple question, I realized had been answered falsely for so long that it was very confusing.

"Well actually all of a sudden I feel okay," I said jokingly. We both smiled.

"But, uh lately," I swallowed hard. "I haven't quite felt myself."

My first of many tears began to fall uncontrollably. Here I was with so much to say but nothing to say all at the same time.

"I've been sad lately," was all I could muster.

> *I am a black woman.*
> *I am strong.*
> *I have large warm open outstretched arms ready to hold you.*
> *I have large breast soft as pillows ready for you to lie your heavy head upon.*

A picture in my mind formed of me in my bed still in my pajamas in the middle of the day. That picture turned into a movie. A movie I replayed over and over again. A movie of me in bed day after day, not wanting and not having the strength to even bathe. I went days without getting out of bed for anything unless I had to.

My kids would knock on the door come in and climb into bed with me. They would lie there heads on my chest and ask me what's wrong. I would whisper a hoarse, "Mommy doesn't feel well." It was true. I didn't know what was wrong. I just knew I didn't feel good. I didn't feel like myself. Thoughts exhausted me. Like the thought of getting up and going to the restroom or the thought of eating. All of those simple things took so much effort and energy that I just didn't have.

"I feel tired all the time. I don't want to get out of bed. I guess I just feel alone," I advised.
I hadn't realized that my voice had trailed off until she cleared her throat to speak again.
"Tell me about what's going on in your life right now," she said.

I am a black woman.
I am strong.
I have big beautiful lips that spread into a smile as I pour my wisdom and soft kind words into your life.

I smirked because there was a time when I loved to tell people about my life. I was, in my opinion, always doing or planning to do something exciting. For the past 4 years I had been trying very hard to receive my bachelor's degree. I worked very hard. I had a lot to prove to a lot of people including myself. I needed to show them that I was not a failure and that I could finish something I started. But here I was one semester from finishing and I had run out of financial aid and hope. At this point I was very exhausted of school and really did want to quit but then that would prove everyone was right. I was a failure.

I think she realized that I didn't have the words to answer that question so she said, "Tell me about a typical day for Candace." I smiled again but I don't know why.

"Well, lately it's just been me waking up every day and a lot of times arguing with myself and my bed, pillows, and blankets on rather or not I will get out of bed and why. The bed, blankets, and pillows usually wins." We both laughed.

I shrugged my shoulders saying, "I guess I just feel tired. I feel like my body, mind, and spirit is exhausted and just needs rest." I rolled my eyes and shook my head to avoid more tears spilling.
Those words sounded ridiculous coming out of my mouth.

"Do you not feel like you deserve to rest? What I mean to say is this, why is Candace taking time to get rest a problem," she asked.

I laughed a full Candace laugh that made snot burst out of my running nose. She smiled and casually passed me a Kleenex tissue. I wiped away more tears and blew my nose.

I am a black woman.
I am strong.
I am wise.
There is nothing I cannot do.

Now, how was I, a black woman, supposed to sit here and explain to this white woman why I felt it was so unacceptable for me to think that it was okay to just sit around and do nothing?

You see, I'm not just a black woman. I'm a single black mother with little to no help form my children's fathers. If I **don't do** then it **don't** get done and **that** is **unacceptable**.

I may be allowed to have a day. That's one day. But this little issue I'd been having had been going on so long that I'd sort of lost track of time.
"Well, I just feel that given my situation I really can't afford to sit around and do nothing. As a single mother if I don't do what needs to be done than it just doesn't get done and that is not acceptable."

I am a black woman.
I am strong.
I work hard.
I love hard.

"You know a lot of women deal with this same issue. Some are married, some are not married. Women are naturally givers. We give and give and give until we have nothing left. But I warn you: If you don't give something to yourself: time, rest, love or whatever you need to keep giving you will burn out. If you don't take care of Candace then you will never be able to take care of anyone else and yes that includes your children. Candace, you deserve to be rewarded sometimes for the effort you put forth in this life. Those rewards don't have to be big or expensive. It's the tiny things that we deny ourselves of that can make such a huge impact on our everyday life. Things such as taking a short nap, leaving the dishes until tomorrow. Actually taking the time to enjoy a conversation with our friends without feeling guilty about not doing the long list of things that will always be there waiting for us when were done," she proclaimed.

I listened very closely and I recognized that everything she said was true. And honestly it did make me feel good to hear her say it was okay. But images in my mind played so clearly of the life I would have to return to once I left this office. Right now, it kind of felt good, safe even, to sit here with this woman and share and get acknowledgement of my feelings but the reality is, that when this was over and yes it would be, I would have to return to Candace. And Candace is alone.

It's a force to be reckoned with.
It is always around me.
It's an energy that I feel like a warm blanket but it's cold.
It lingers.
I don't always know what it is but I always know it's there.

I drove away from her office in silence. No radio. No CD's in the CD player. I even silenced my phone. No distractions. It was time to really face me. I didn't want to go home right away, I wasn't ready for that, so I drove the familiar distance to a familiar place I'd come to often just to get away. A park I felt was forgotten by most had become my favorite place in the world. There wasn't much to this park. The grass was often overgrown. The swing set rusted and the slide was bent. There were one or two benches whose legs had sunken into the ground. I would often walk past all of that to a little dock that stretched a small ways across the St. Johns River. I cried to this great body of water at the end of its dock many days. I could always cry my ugly cry here. Who would laugh? Who would the river tell? And afterward I would wipe my face and return to my world as if nothing had ever happened.

I'd only brought one other person here. This place was special to me and so was he. Not perfect, but special just like this park.

Today I pulled in knowing that when I would leave things would definitely be different in my life. I'd left her office resolved about some things and for the first time in a long time I knew that I was different and that no matter what I would leave town. I didn't know where I was going or how I was going to get there but it was time for a fresh start. The entire idea wasn't new for me. I'd planned to leave for years but there was always something or some reason to stay. Today my mind was made up.

I parked the car in my normal spot and turned it off. I pulled down the sun visor and lifted the cover of the mirror. I stared at me and smiled. I looked around and realized just like this park with it's over grown lawn and plain exterior, that although it wasn't perfect it was special because my times here had made it special. My tears, my fears, my imperfections, and my honesty in this one spot made it special for me. I loved it all and

I love all of me. It was special and so am I.

The Vow That I Made... To Me

By: Dionne Brunson

Dionne Brunson
FOOTBALL SHEOLOGY FOUNDER

dionnebrunson@outlook.com
www.FootballSheology.com

There are so many women like me who have tried way too hard to keep their depression a secret. That, alone, can be depressing. The daily self-assessment I had to do was grueling. And I often did it all alone and unsure about whether my loved ones could understand what I was going through. There is way too little education about depression and the role it plays in our families. There are still too many people that don't even believe depression is real.

My sincere prayer is that we, as women, learn that there is a fine line between being strong and being self-destructive. That we find the right balance between embracing our flaws and owning our strengths. I believe that balance is a sacred place for us. That small space is where our youth meets our wisdom, where the old becomes new and where we evolve from girls to women. We spent our early years making good and bad decisions, learning from our peers, watching our friends and getting to know ourselves. Those things are what assist in molding our maturation process and contributes to the wisdom we grow into.

My bout with depression is not my whole story. It's merely a small piece of me that I've learned to embrace. I want you to embrace every part of your life also. I don't want any of you to feel ashamed or embarrassed by any piece of you. I want you to understand that there is a big difference between your life and your life situations. Your life situations do not have final say in the life you create for yourself.

My twenties were a complete lie. I spent most of that time trying to convince almost everyone I came in contact with that I was mentally, financially, and spiritually stable. That I had everything going for myself. I tried to wear the right clothes, say the right things, excel in my career, be the right kind of daughter, and be the perfect mother. Somehow and somewhere along the way I fell victim to the notion that the perfect woman aimed to please everyone around her. I believed that being nurturing, supportive, and motherly had everything to do with pleasing everyone around me. Trying to be perfect in every way is way too much pressure for one person to bear. Having an incessant need to please everyone takes you to a point where you're good at trying. However, you certainly don't become perfect at pleasing people because that's an impossible feat. But I became perfect in the act of trying. It's something I inadvertently practiced every single day. I became the leading actress in my own stage play entitled "YES". I became, to a fault, a professional "yes woman" to everyone that I was in direct contact with. The gross reality to my self-appointed position is that the more I said yes to others, the more I said "no" to myself. The very essence of me was slowly slipping away. It's hard to pin point where it started, how it progressed or where the scale became so imbalanced. I couldn't even tell you the point where other people became more important than me. Looking back on it I just know that it was a learned behavior and I wasn't even conscious of it being something that could be detrimental to my health and especially to my life. That practice lead me to a lonely and dark place. Eventually it took me on a one way road to a bout of depression.

I often hear people describe depression in a way similar to sinking into a dark hole. It sometimes felt like that for me. But most of the time it felt like standing still in the middle of Times Square all while life was happening all around me. But I felt paralyzed, unable to move, or make decisions. Whenever I tried to move or get out of life's way I'd jump right into the path of a an oncoming train. I can't say for sure that trying to please everyone is the direct cause for my depression. Though I can say with the utmost confidence that trying to please everyone highly contributed to putting me on the fast track to having depression.

The self-destructive thought process of trying to make everyone happy and forgetting about myself wasn't a coincidence. It came from 20 years of thinking that's the right way to gain acceptance. I saw that behavior all around me. I can remember as far back as first grade believing that making others happy gave me a sense of fulfillment. It was almost as if I accomplished something worthwhile by making someone else happy. Ironically, I spent most of my youth feeling like it was impossible to actually make those around me happy. But I continuously tried.

My childhood wasn't much different than many young women of today. I was raised by an exceptional single mother and barely a father. It's unfortunate, but I too am a part of that group of women who are forced together by the commonality of either barely having a father or not having one in her life at all. There are way too many of us. The outline of our life stories are often the same but our individual chapters have a uniqueness that defines women like us for years to come.

My outline starts and ends with my mother. She has always been the person who wouldn't think twice about giving me her last. Like so many single mothers she literally had to scrape and save every penny she earned just to feed and clothe me. She traveled with me every chance she had. She showed me parts of life that helped me to open my mind and see the world through other people's struggles and perspectives. But she also carried the weight of far too many burdens that any one woman should see in just one lifetime. I have heard stories of things she's gone through. I saw some of her burdens first hand. Till this day, when my Mom nonchalantly talks about some of her tribulations I hear the enormity of what she had gone through. Sometimes I even felt her burdens as if they were my own because for a long time it was just she and I. We took care of each other physically, mentally and emotionally. I wanted, so badly, to protect her from her worries.

Our relationship dynamic usually worked for us and was often a good thing. Other times, taking care of each other kind of blurred the lines of identity for me. Obviously she knew she was the Mother between her and me. For me it wasn't always that clear. There were many days I wanted so badly to make everything better for my Mom. I have memories that go back to grade school of me wanting to fix my Mothers problems. Wanting to be her savior was also another avenue for me to practice pleasing another person.

My biological father spent most of my youth chasing women and making five children with five different women. I've been told there are more of us out there. It wouldn't surprise me and I'd sort of expect it. He's still alive and doing well I presume. He prefers not to be a part of my life. There was a time that I wanted him to be a stand up man and tell me why he chose to be absent. It made me angry for far too long that I wasn't good enough to be his daughter. Or at the very least be worth some sort of explanation. As a child I had no idea how to deal with the situation. I was too young and immature to rationalize the idea that a father didn't want to be a part of his daughter's life. And as an adult I learned it was not worth trying to rationalize that idea but rather to learn how to deal with. It wasn't until somewhere around my 35th birthday that I realized his actions are not something I should try to understand. My job was simply to let go, forgive him and move on. Not having a father does something to the psyche of a young woman. For me it made me question my worth. It also made me unsure about my value. I couldn't tell if I was being a bad daughter or if he just wasn't a good

Father. That's not something a child should be confused about.

Not having my father in my life was a traumatizing thing for me as a young woman. And on top of that I had a stepfather who was a heroin addict most of my youth. He eventually went away to a rehabilitation hospital when I was 11 years old and he beat his addiction after many attempts. Soon after, I legally and happily took on his last name as my own. Technically he was my stepfather but treated me no different than if I were biologically his. At least that's what I believe. I can't say for certain I know what it feels like to have an inborn unconditional love from a biological father. I can only speak to what I experienced. And I believe my stepfather was my father in the very literal sense of the word. Even through his addiction he helped take care of me. I loved him like crazy. Yet there was always an unexplainable void. I knew it and I think he knew it also. Eventually, even after his sobriety, his addiction caught up to all of us. He was diagnosed as being HIV positive and having liver cancer. He passed away when I was 17 years old. I have comfort in that I was able to experience the joys of having a father for six years. I also have sadness in that I've had no father for 34 years and counting.

By the time I was 19 years old I had two daughters, no husband, a rocky relationship with my mother, no father I could turn to, and nothing short of a certified dysfunctional extended family. Adding insult to injury was that I also had very little confidence in my future. I carried all of this baggage in addition to my lack of identity and low self-esteem which culminated in me pretending to be okay. I pretended for almost ten years. Those negative demons I carried reared their ugly little heads somewhere around my 28th birthday.

I became fed up. Mentally, everything was just too much to bear. I knew I couldn't continue to bust my ass trying to satisfy everyone. It seemed like every time I tried to take better care of my mental self those around me just weren't accepting of my change. My world started to get smaller and smaller. Those brittle walls surrounding what little self-esteem and confidence I had crumbled. I had run myself into a brick wall and couldn't go any further.

My body and my brain just stopped. I was emotionally, spiritually and physically tapped out. I reached my wits end and had nowhere to turn. I honestly believed a coffin buried six feet underground was an easy solution. My doctor prescribed me to participate in "voluntary" aggressive outpatient mental therapy. It was voluntary in the sense that if I didn't attend she would commit me to an inpatient program against my will. I had no choice but to participate.

It wasn't as bad as it may seem. The experience taught me the most important thing about myself at that time. I learned I had no idea who I was, who I wanted to be or what I wanted out of life. It was scary because I also had no idea how to figure it out. So much of my life, up to that point, was spent trying to make others happy so they would accept me but I never really accepted myself. I had to figure out how to do that.

The second most important thing I learned is that I've never really quite fit in anywhere. I can't think of a time where I felt like I completely belonged to a group of people. Outside of my Mother, Husband and children I've never completely belonged to a functional family. There are groups of friends, churches I belonged to, organizations I contributed my time to and even parts of my own family that I wanted to be accepted into. It just never worked out that way.

I knew if I wanted to be genuinely happy with myself I had to tackle those two things head on. I needed to find out who I was and I needed to be okay with not being a part of a familial unit. Funny how those tables turned. Especially since everything I did before this epiphany was solely to gain acceptance. Now I was forcing myself to stand on my own without having approval from others.

I vowed to do three things to get myself on the right track. I knew if I (1) got a better understanding of who I was, (2) determined the type of woman I wanted to be and (3) learned to receive the blessings set aside for me then the rest would fall in place. Those three tasks essentially gave me a better sense of myself while embracing my past and prepared me for my future.

I began to focus on myself whole heartedly. I found ways to essentially date myself all by myself. I even used my commute to and from work to have conversations with myself. I talked about things I liked and didn't like. I spoke out loud to myself about things I wanted to change and things I wanted to embrace. For probably the first time in my life I started listening to myself. I listened to my wants and needs. I paid better attention to my internal reactions of what I was telling myself. Good reactions meant positive things. Uncomfortable reactions made my antennae's go up as something I needed to be more cautious of.

My personal conversations evolved into making lists. I wrote lists about my favorite hobbies, books I'd like to read, websites I wanted to visit, places I wanted to go, and many other things. Some lists included intangible tasks such as appreciate the small things, be more in the moment, and replace negative thoughts with positive thoughts. I still make lists on a monthly basis. I have a notebook full of lists and I refer to them often. They're like little reminders to keep focus on me in my busy life.

Eventually my lists evolved to actions items. I became anxious to try new things and see results. I started to be able to cross off items on those lists. I'd pick tasks and made them weekly and monthly goals. Even when I fell short of accomplishing a task or goal I learned to forgive myself. I had to teach myself to embrace my failures instead of being ashamed of them. I learned to simply begin again.

Nowadays my thoughts have more wisdom in them. I think differently. I feel more intently. I believe with purpose. I love unconditionally. I'm confident there are very few things I can't accomplish with time and dedication. I've been successful with some things and I've failed at others. I don't let my successes give me exaggerated hope no more than I let my fears slow me down. I know I'm not the perfect wife, daughter, or mother. And I'm okay with that. I no longer try to be. I know that my shortcomings are not failures but rather that I have space to grow and more things to learn. I've felt the maturity and wisdom steadily rising and growing inside of me over the past ten years. It's almost like I've been giving birth to this beautiful baby called LIFE. The best way I can describe my life right now is to say that every step I take and every task I complete is like a star in the night sky shining bright. Eventually all of my stars will form into full blown constellations that I have yet to fully imagine.

By: Candace Smith

It's a force to be reckoned with. It is always around me. It's an energy that I feel like a warm blanket. It's never not there even when a smile is on my face. It lingers. I don't always know what it is but I always know it's there. It's a voice so loud that it's silent. A deafening noise that screams every hurtful and mean thought I've ever had over and over louder and louder until that's all I hear. And on the rare occasion that I get a chance to hear something nice, or sweet or positive it's Spanish. It's foreign. It's unbelievable. It's new. It's fresh. It's a vacation. But vacations don't last. That's why they're called vacations. It's a break from the norm. That's what positivity is to me. It's a vacation. It's not real life. Real life is cold, tiresome, hard, frustrating. It's mostly losses instead of wins, its more tears and a lot less smiles. It's more anger. It's a lot of phoniness and exhausting pretending. That's why I wanna sleep all day. To dream about what life should be like. To remember the days when I wasn't so tired and I didn't need a jump from some other positive energy source. I was my own positive energy source. I had so much positive energy I could jump start anybody. Your battery could have been dead for ten years but ten minutes with me and you'd be back on the road. I miss her. I miss her energy. I miss her life. I miss her smile. I miss her sincere, head all the way back, stomach hurt, almost about to pee in her clothes laugh. It's rare. It's an endangered species.
I miss me.

Sticks and Stones

By: D. Elaine Wiggins

D. Elaine Wiggins
delaine.wiggins@gmail.com

When I decided to participate in this project, I asked myself, "What could I have told my younger self that may have helped me?" I know unless someone has been through the same thing, it's hard to hear them. I want you to know that I understand what it feels like to be so afraid that when you open your mouth to speak fear grips you and no words come out. I know what it feels like to walk through a building full of adults with all this authority and power, as I saw it as a child, and feel unworthy of its use to protect me. To feel the huge world around me but notice my limited access to move about it freely and safely. To feel left out or to be in a crowd but having mastered the art of being invisible, because if no one notices you, you are safe from hurt. To be silent even when you want and need to speak. Or to have others say 'SPEAK UP", but you don't feel you can.

I can recall years ago having to sing in front of many people for the first time. I opened my mouth in fear and nothing came out because I was so afraid.

I didn't even understand what I was afraid of. I had mastered the art of being invisible for so long that I didn't know how to respond when seen. I overcame that fear by the help of my Pastor Kenneth Middleton and First Lady Lisa Middleton, who continued to "push me" up front. They vowed to not allow me to hide my gift. It is people like them that I'm now so thankful to God for, they helped to inspire me to want to be to someone what they were to me.

I learned at that moment that sometimes you don't even realize how some things may have affected your life until you are challenged in a certain area. I had been reprogrammed not to do anything that would draw attention to myself. When I left high school I'd truly began to embrace my self-worth, it was and continues to be a journey that I am enjoying. It is a wonderful thing when you truly begin to even grasp the level of worth, love, and value God has placed on you.

I would say to young women who may be in any challenging situation to move toward those things that respond to your true value and away from that which does not. Please know that one of your most powerful weapons is your voice and you must use it. Know that this whole project is done with you in mind. I hope this helps you to realize that no matter what you go through it will not last forever. Nothing stays the same in life and that you do have the power to affect that change! We care about you!

Its Friday afternoon, a cloudy, hot and humid 92 degrees outside, with the heat drawing most of my energy from me; but the fear of getting on the school bus compelled in comparison. The atmosphere was filled with the sounds of children laughing. Playful screams poured from the buses as other students lined one behind the other. However, I remembered to walk as far away from the buses as possible, in anticipation that again, Larry would throw something out at me since he'd always done so. He had been in every class with me since my very first day of school. I remember it like it was yesterday.

I was a shy little 6 year old. Never having been in a daycare or any other setting with other children, except at home with my 7 other siblings. I was so nervous that day and since there wasn't a teacher in the classroom yet I sat in the first empty seat that I saw. Suddenly, I heard the loud screeching sound of a chair against the tile floor. A curly haired, brown eyed boy, who was much bigger than any other first grader in our class, jumped up from his seat, stormed over and pushed me out of my chair. "That's *MY* seat," he said angrily. I got up from the floor, straightened the ruffles on my little dress and moved to another seat in the back of the class.

As the years progressed so did Larry's behavior. Grade after grade his behavior grew more tormenting. Time progressed and with every passing year my plan was consistent, to *"survive in school"*. I had already spent most of this year in school struggling between listening to my teacher, Mr. Johnson, while trying to block out the degrading insults Larry continuously whispered from the seat behind me, "Stupid. Stank self. You just wait until I see you by yourself umma!" He never said what he would do but my imagination ran fearfully wild. He'd go on and on. His words stabbing like a dagger. "Old dumb self," he spewed. In between the verbal torture there were small items thrown at me whenever the teacher would turn to the board to write. He would suck his teeth whenever I answered a question. For which I started doing less and less of, instead, I'd found myself fading in and out of thoughts of how I could escape this life with him in it. I imagined myself standing up to him and what would happen. I thought of going to my parents or the school principal but then surely he would be called into the office which would only make him angrier with me.

During the school year Sunday evenings were the worst. I would spend Sunday's stressing about how to survive the week of misery to come. I wondered what it felt like to be excited about school. I would see students who were involved in school activities and wished I had that freedom. I'd always wanted to be in the Spelling Bee but instead I sat in the audience year after year, quietly and correctly spelling words that were called.

As I stood thinking about those days a slimy piece of wet paper comes flying out of the bus window at me and landed on my bare arm. I was disgusted and humiliated as I wiped it off quickly looking long enough to see it was him who'd thrown it. I never looked him in his face long, as not to appear to challenge him. But instead I embarrassingly looked around in hopes no one else noticed except maybe one of the teachers, who could intervene, but as usual, that intervention never came. I was always quiet natured, talented, and wise with an inner strength that for a long time I was not aware of. While I had seen school days end this way many times before, today seemed different in some way. Briefly I glance over and see his face still fixed at the open bus window, staring at me. "Betta not get on this bus," he says the moment I look at him. With that look in his eyes, the one I had seen so many times before, the one that was cold, downright evil. The look of something impure and non-childlike. I felt that I was no match for it. As I walked defeated I noticed one of my teachers who was very aware of the bullying I suffered from him glance at me with pity. Then she walked away without a word, she didn't save me like I had expected. With such a somber feeling the weather shifted to match my mood. It started to drizzle. I had walked those couple miles in the rain before but today was not the same as any other day. In a single moment I had grown different. I questioned myself loudly within. "Why?"

All but one bus was left loading when something rose up in me. I couldn't identify whether it was anger, hurt, or humiliation. A bold fearlessness sprung up. I turned moving hurriedly towards the bus. "Where are you going," someone asked. "I'm getting on the bus!" I said sternly. As I stormed quickly onto the bus I took 3 steps up, but then I looked back at the students in their seats staring, all eyes were on me. I saw Larry gleaning towards me with that hateful look in his eyes. Suddenly, I didn't feel so bold any more. I immediately turned and sat on the door way steps of the bus. I looked back at the kind face of Mrs. Marvell, the bus driver, for approval, she gently smiled and said, "It's ok." She never said much else after that. She seemed to possess a quiet strength and I knew I would be safe next to her. Fear eased as the bus door closed in front of me. Then, there was that screeching sound of the wheels that I'd heard so often from the outside, a jolt of the bus, and it was moving. Soon the same old playful sounds that poured out the windows so many times before, faded into the background. As I watched the trees fly by and the wet ground roll under my feet from the bottom doorway steps of the bus. I felt good inside. Not sure if it was the bus ride or the strength I felt when I decided to get on it.

The following year everything changed. For once in my life school was not a place of horror. I felt like a normal, happy teenager and it was the only year I had not seen Larry in class. I heard he went to another school just outside of the city, but wherever he was, I was just happy he was not there. The school term finally ended and I'd done well all year.

The summer after my torment, I decided to do something that I had never done. I decided to participate in our city's annual festival. I definitely didn't feel I was cute enough, however, I felt I needed to do this, I owed it to myself. The day of the event I was both excited and nervous. Then while standing back stage, I began to look around at the other models, and suddenly my insecurities began to speak me. "You are not pretty like these other girls," were the sounds that rang in my ears. "There are over a thousand people out there, what if they laugh at you?" I become even more nervous but this time fear became fuel. I told myself, "You *can* do this." I'd practiced all summer for this moment and had the right to walk this stage no matter what anyone thought or said, including '*my own voice of insecurities.*' I did just that and it was an amazing feeling! I was not skinny, the cutest, nor the best dressed on that stage, but what meant the most to me was that I was there.

Summer break was over and I entered high school optimistic about the year ahead. I might try out to be a cheerleader this year, I think as I settle confidently at my desk. Just when the feeling that this would be another good year came in mind in walks Larry! I couldn't believe he was back! Where the heck did he come from? He had grown too. He was taller and bigger. He appeared to be about 5'9 looking at minimum 200 pounds of meanness!

I fully expected him to say something to me and sure enough he eventually did. Later that day Mr. Leslie, my English teacher asked a question, as I had done for the past few years. I answered it correctly, suddenly Larry sucks his teeth and attempts to shift his oversized body in his seat and look back at me. Nearly everyone knew our history. All you could hear was Mr. Leslie's chalk writing my answer on the board .Then the class became consumed by a loud silence. I looked him directly in his eyes and for the first time I was not afraid of him. I did not feel that feeling of oppression that came over me while in his presence for so many years. In fact, he almost looked weak to me and for lack of a better description, I want to say I felt sorry for him.

His stare was no longer frightening. Maybe because mine was more powerful. In a moment I saw his insecurities. Within seconds his cold stare, the one that he'd used to intimidate me for years, grew curious and weaker. The surprise in his eyes danced and studied me all over, before his eyes retreated. He then turned himself back around in his seat without a word. It was the last time he had ever looked to bother me again. Now I realize that all the prayers I prayed as a young child, asking God to "make him stop" and hoping that my victimizer would change, it may never have happened, because the change I needed was not in him but instead it was in me. I had the power all along to bend life in my favor. God had already told me who I was. That I was created with purpose on purpose and I would never forget that.

I now realize that childhood is a time in life when you are fragile and developing. That during that time the opportunity for life's challenges to redefine who you believe you are through the actions of others are great. I learned through this involvement not just to leave the door open for my own children but to go through the door to them and ask specific questions about how they are doing and feeling. This experience taught me to encourage them to feel free to speak to me about anything.

Because of my childhood I have made sure to tell my own children and any other child, as regularly as possible how valuable they are. That I care about what happens to them and will intervene where it is needed. I remind them that they have a right to speak out. They should expect and even demand a safe transition through their childhood. To speak up if they don't like the way someone makes them feel. Rather it's a touch, a word, or a look. I encourage them to use the most powerful tool that they have... their voice. And keep using it until they find someone who will hear. Because sooner or later someone will hear.

What Glitters.. Isn't Always Gold

By: Emily Hendrickson

Emily Hendrickson
Erb36575@gmail.com

It wasn't hard for me to come up with something to write for The Exodus Project because I live with the main parts of my story daily, my beautiful children. Although my story isn't what I had "dreamed" of as a little girl, the Lord has still blessed me through it all and he will you too.

As you read through my story I pray that it will help you overcome some of the obstacles you may be facing. Know that you are a STRONG and BEAUTIFUL creation of God and he will love you through it.

Being a single mother was one of THE hardest things I have ever done. But, it was also the most rewarding thing in the end. Remember that no matter WHAT you're overcoming, get on your knees and remember who made you. Find your worth in HIM, the Lord our God. Love your children unconditionally and with your whole heart. Even when you can barely take another step, take it for them. Remember they are only little once.

"But from there you will seek the Lord your God and you will find him, if you search after him with all your heart and with all your soul." –Deuteronomy 4:29

As a child I can remember the turbulent existence that I had just like it was yesterday. Although I knew that things were not supposed to be so difficult, I never imagined that the choices that were made would affect my future. There were a lot of changes in my life that I think, ultimately, had huge impacts on some of the choices I made. The good ones and the bad ones. Multiple divorces (between both parents), step siblings coming and going, moves to different homes, schools and towns. I am certainly not blaming my parents for all of my choices. However, we must take into account that one's upbringing impacts who he or she becomes.

I met my high school sweetheart during my junior year. We were together from junior year until after graduation. I was madly in love with him. We had a close enough relationship that we were sleeping together and I would even stay at his home with him and his family. We were inseparable. I honestly thought he was the one that I was meant to spend the rest of my life with. In 2001, after 3 years together, he broke off our relationship. I am still to this day not quite sure what the reason was and I struggle with that uncertainty. I remember how cold and unapologetic he was and it broke my heart to the point I couldn't breathe. I remember dropping to my knees in his front yard sobbing uncontrollably. I was in that state for a good week afterward. After I managed to take a breath and actually start eating and breathing properly again, I decided to move on. AOL (America Online) was very popular at the time and I decided to check out one of the chat rooms to lift my spirits. While in one of the chatrooms, a guy started showing me some interest. We became friends online and chatted for a few days. Through our conversations I found out he didn't live far from me; so we decided to meet one night at a gas station. Now that I think of it, it is NOT safe to meet a guy you met online at a gas station by yourself, especially at night. He was cute, we flirted a lot. He had a house, a car, and owned his own business.

After about a week of flirting and chatting I found myself so smitten with the attention he was giving me that I decided to be intimate with him. This is a decision I would regret the rest of my life. All it takes is one time to get pregnant and that's exactly how I ended up. It's amazing how a person can paint a picture of who they wished that they were. He turned out to be NONE of the things he portrayed himself to be. He lied about owning a home. He lied about owning a business. He lied about everything else that came out of his mouth. The truth was that he lived with his alcoholic mother and step-father, 28 dogs, and 14 cats. All which were housed in a single wide trailer. Here I was 20 years old and freshly out of high school and now pregnant. I was brokenhearted and looking for attention in a rebound relationship and boy did I get it. I was so angry at myself for not having more self-worth and getting myself in this horrible situation.

I didn't tell him that I was pregnant. I decided that I would raise this baby on my own with my family. It seemed like a great plan until my mom and step-dad got into a huge argument about my situation and split up. Although there were other issues in the relationship I took it personally. I felt so hopeless. I got in my car and I drove out to his mother's trailer in the country. I was 5 months pregnant and showing. Tonight I was going to break the news to him. To my surprise they were ecstatic and over the moon. Supposedly, he couldn't have kids due to a low sperm count. I definitely wished that was the case. I held my shoulders back and with as much courage as I could muster told him he had to get a job and man up to his responsibility. We needed a house or apartment, items for the baby, and a more reliable vehicle. He agreed and things were okay for a little while. It only took me a month to determine that I had made a mistake by telling him that I was pregnant and going there to live. He was verbally abusive. He screamed at me, it seemed that this was the norm because he fought with his family as well. The environment was hectic, his family was drunk every single day and he refused to get a job. He stole money from his mother's bank account and blamed me. I was miserable and I was drained mentally, emotionally, and spiritually.

As if I didn't have enough negative things happening I found out when I was 6 months along that something was wrong with my baby. The doctor could see from the ultrasounds that his bowels were distended and swollen and couldn't quite tell me what was going on with him or why. I was told that I would have to wait until he was born and they could give me more options for treatment when they could physically assess them. This news was enough to send me over the edge and spiral me into major anxiety and depression. Everything in life seemed abnormal. I wanted to run but I couldn't because he wouldn't let me leave him. He wouldn't let me call my family or go return home. I felt like I was being held hostage.

Because of the stressful environment I delivered my son at 37 weeks. At the time of his birth he was diagnosed with Jejunal Atresia. When he was 3 days old he had 28 inches of his intestines removed. He stayed in the NICU for almost a month. I had the opportunity to get away from him at that point. I returned home with my mom and step-dad. I went to the NICU every single day for his duration there and I stayed there from morning until they would kick me out. The father of my son never came and never asked to come see the baby. I now see that as a blessing even though it hurt like hell at the time. When I was able to bring my baby home, I was very grateful for my mother's help. She helped me more than anyone. Honestly, I don't think that I would've made it without her.

When my parents relocated I took on the financial responsibility of subleasing the apartment. After their departure I grew lonely and heartbroken. I felt like I was missing something. My child's father started coming around and telling me he finally wanted to be a daddy.

I was so lonely that I believed every sweet talking word that man muttered to me. I was blinded and foolish. When the lease was up on the apartment, like a fool, I moved back into the trailer with him and his alcoholic dysfunctional family. I desperately longed for a family, a mother and a father for my child. I wanted it so badly that I put my integrity and his well-being on the line at the time. Things there did not get better. Along with him not working, mooching off of and stealing from his mother, and treating me like dirt; he started forcing me to have sex with him.

There was definitely a disconnect between the two of us. I didn't like him at all but I stayed there to ensure that my son had both of his parents under one roof. The beginning of my last days there began on the night that I found an instant message that he had received. I looked at it and noticed that it was from a girl and it was very flirty and forward. While he was in the shower I sat down and read it and decided to take it upon myself to inform her that he wasn't technically single and had a new son. He came out of the shower and saw what I was doing and became enraged. He pushed me out of the chair onto the floor. I didn't have far to fall because we were in a little travel camper beside his mom's single wide. He started deleting things on the computer like that would erase what just occurred. While he was yelling and lashing out at me I grabbed the baby from where he was sleeping and tried to run. He caught me at the door before I could get out and proceeded to try to take the baby from my arms. We fought for a few minutes and finally I was able to get out the door. I ran into his mom's house and into her bedroom while he chased me yelling. I stayed with her that night and waited until morning to figure out what to do next. I knew I had to get out and I desperately searched for a way to do it safely. I went to my mom's house the next day and moved back in with them. I never did tell them what happened because I had burned so many bridges with their trust. I was looking through rose colored glasses and I saw what I thought was love.

Several days passed and I called him to see about coming over to get the things that I had left behind. He agreed I could and said it would be civil. While I was packing my things he proceeded to try to talk me into staying, I told him that I was not going to stay. I was trying to learn from my mistakes. All I could envision was my son. He was my number one priority. When I tried to leave he wouldn't let me go. He sicced the dogs on me and had them standing in attack mode between me and the exit door. I sat in the back room on the phone with 911 for about 30 minutes while we all tried to talk him into letting me leave. There were police officers surrounding the perimeter of the property trying to talk him into being smart and not making things worse for himself. I had to make him a promise that I wouldn't press charges against him if he let me leave unharmed. I walked across the longest half acre of land to get out of the fence, but I got out.

About a month had passed and I had moved on. Unfortunately, just when I thought all of that was behind me I found out I was pregnant again and he was the father. I was devastated. My oldest son was only 6 months old when I found out I was 2 months pregnant. Here I was 21 years old and was in this situation again. I absolutely couldn't believe it. The difference this time was that I didn't go back to him. I WASN'T going to go back to him. I COULDN'T go back to him. I was better than that and my babies were far more important to me. I stayed at my mom's house and with her help I gave birth to my second son 15 months after my first.

I didn't tell my children's father that I had my second son. He found out somehow and he started accusing me of being a whore and proclaiming that neither of my children were his. Boy, what a blessing from the Lord that turned out to be. He never gave me money and he never came to visit. He never bothered me or the kids again. He was out of our lives. I couldn't imagine being forced to send my children to an abusive freeloader and his alcoholic family every other weekend. That would have been devastating. God was in control. Although I made some terrible mistakes he had us in the palm of his hands the whole time. Those little blessings were meant to be here and I was meant to be their mother. Birthing those beautiful babies made me stronger. I was more confident in myself than ever before.

My mom and step-dad ended up finding some land in Texas they wanted to buy and had decided to move there. I asked if I could come. I just wanted a fresh start. I packed me and my children, along with all that I owned and followed them 14 hours away to a foreign place with lots of hope in my heart. The boys were now 2 months and 17 months old. I stayed with my mom at her house until I could secure a job and get a place of my own. Which I did, along with putting my two little ones in daycare, and working hard for everything I had. It felt really good. I got involved in church and a year later was married to a musician I met while at the church. We have been married for 10 years and now have 5 boys in our brood.

Those boys never missed their "dad". They never knew what happened and that was the Lords protection on their lives for which I will forever be grateful. They are now 11 and almost 13 and are very smart, handsome boys. Their dad still doesn't try to make contact or form a relationship and for that I'm still thankful. He has other kids now and he's married. He lives with her parents. The Lord continues to protect us from that situation. Although my life is far from perfect and I am not certain what is in store for me and my children in the future. I can always rest in his hands and know that he loves us despite our sometimes bad choices. That he will be that "void" that I thought I had to fill with a man. He's such a better choice than any other I could ever make.

Break Up To Make Up... With Me

By: Erica Ware

THE BIG GIRL MOVEMENT FOUNDER

AUTHOR OF THE BROWN GIRL BLUES

imtheconfidencecoach@gmail.com

Dear Sister,

I know exactly what it's like to experience heartache, and wonder if I'll ever attain love again. You're with this person that you know without a doubt, that you'll be with them forever. And in an instant they're gone. Sometimes with no real explanation. It happens to women every day. We enter relationships with the mindset that this is forever, and something traumatic happens and it's over in a millisecond.

I'm writing you today to assure you that life does indeed go on. I acknowledge that in this moment you probably can't see the light at the end of the tunnel. But it's there. Shining bold, bright and ready for you to grab it. You have to dig deep inside yourself, and Go somewhere you've never been.

I wrote this story with each and every woman in mind who's struggling with finding their place in life after heartbreak. For every woman who believed in a fairytale dream type of love, and had to abruptly wake up. This story is for us. Just the reminder you may need to know you can and will push through. Gods speed.

I was happily married to the love of my life, or so I thought. We spent 10 great years together off and on. However, much like most things we go through in life, our season was abruptly over. I was devastated. I was beyond devastated. I fell into an extremely deep depression. I isolated myself from family, friends, and all of my favorite things. I even took a back seat on running my business. I thought my marriage was forever. I made the mistake of thinking my happiness was actually in my marriage; however I was quickly reminded that MY happiness was in me.

I remember one day, on my way out to run some errands. Pushing through what felt like one of my more bad days, during this ugly depression, I caught a glimpse of myself in the mirror. Although, I felt completely broken on the inside, it never showed on my exterior. I've always took extreme pride in my appearance. In that moment, the Creator spoke to me, through my reflection. I vividly heard him say, "Erica, you are so much more worthy than anything that doesn't add value to your life. You're beautiful both inside and out. A love that you deserve in its entirety will come. Be patient." It seemed like in that very moment, I remembered who I was. I felt the pep immediately back in my step. I felt rejuvenated in my broken soul. I felt stronger than I have ever felt in my life. I stopped isolating myself from friends, family, and all of my favorite things. And let's be clear, although the Creator spoke directly to me, the process still wasn't easy. It took a shit load of work. SELF WORK. I had to dig deep inside of myself. I had to get to some root problems of my current situation. The very first thing I stopped doing, was blaming her. Yes, no doubt she made the decision to leave and not work on our marriage, but I took responsibility for the things I could have and should have put forth more effort. I realized that when we're the "victim" or someone leaves a relationship, we tend to try to place all the blame on them. We fail to take any ownership for our behavior. And that's extremely difficult to do when you think you're living in bliss only to find out that you're not. That's why hindsight is 20/20.

The second thing I did was stop living in denial. I plagued myself with thoughts of us reconciling. I just knew this was a rough patch we were going through. Most long term relationships/marriages go through them. But when I finally decided to truly see that she wasn't fighting for us to make it through, I had to tell myself, it's over. It devastated my very being. I had no choice but to persevere. Because the reality was, my life wasn't just about me. People were rooting for me. And more importantly, I had a responsibility to the people who depended on my guidance to pull through. That coupled with the Creator's blatant orders, was my driving force to get myself together.

The third thing I had to do was live my truth. It's not always so simple. Here I am known to the world as being this plus size powerhouse, with a loving partner to match, and now that isn't so. Not only do I have to own this, I have to tell my peers what's currently going on in my life. Every time I told the story, I felt pieces of me being chipped away. I was so embarrassed about my life at that time. Until one day, I was telling someone what happened, and I felt nothing. No emotional ties. No embarrassment. Nothing. It was just like telling any story from your past that you're over. Life as I knew it once again changed, for the better.

The last thing I had to do was detox from her. No texting, no phones. No social media. NO CONTACT of any sort! You can't heal from the very thing that's hurting you if it's still front and center in your life. I had to move on in its entirety. Children included, I had to take my space, for my own sanity. I learned so much about myself through this ugly process. I learned that I had to relearn how to be independent, and self-sufficient. I gave it all up for love. Even myself. That's why when she left, I was completely lost. I didn't leave anything for me. This was a terrible mistake. I didn't conform to who she was at all, but I did get lost along the way. I thought our love was endless, which in turn made me naive. I got comfortable in our situation. I was so comfortable in fact that I couldn't see that my marriage was slipping through the cracks. I couldn't see that in the areas where I had a lackadaisical attitude, I should have had a more progressive one. Oh how we can see things for what they are when we step outside ourselves. The main lesson I learned through this process, was that life truly goes on and it won't wait for you. I allowed myself to grow through the emotions, the hurt and the pain, instead of being stagnant. It bruised me, but I am certainly not broken.

If I Knew Then

By: Gina Perryman

Gina Perryman
ggperryman@gmail.com

Never in a million years would I have imagined that my life would be this way, during this time, on this day, and in this year.

If I had to imagine my life it would be with my mother and me going shopping to welcome my second son. Our days spent with lunch, laughs, and our weekends spent with watching old movies and reading over the Sunday School lesson. But I am not the master of my own destiny. I am just a participant on the roller coaster that we call life.

The day that I lost her was a day that I will never forget. Never have I been in a place where the ultimate strength and the bottom belly of weakness coincided. I have never been more devastated and more vulnerable.

To those that have lost a parent, specifically a mother, I want you to know that there will be days that you can't figure out how you're going to be productive. However, there will be days when you have the best day and you might even feel a bit guilty because for a second you think that you shouldn't forget about her or feel happy. I want to advise you that although life is so different it still seems to go on and so will you.

It hurts. It's unbearable. It's stifling. But you will grow to learn that you have done all that you can and you will become satisfied in knowing that in this moment you are the person that you are specifically because of her. I thank God for allowing my siblings and I to borrow such a magnificent woman to call our own. And I appreciate her for staying here longer so that we would have more time.

Know that you will never forget. But also know that you will become stronger each and every day.

Walk in your strength.

Life has been an uphill battle; I've taken my share of loses. I look at other people and sometimes wonder, "Why do they have it so easy?" There are times I feel like life just gives some folks a pass and wear folks like me down to dust. I've heard all the clichés:

> *"There is a silver lines around every dark cloud!"*
> *"Tough times don't last but tough people do!"*
> *"Night don't last always, Joy comes in the morning!"*
> *"Where there is a will, there is a way!"*

I thought of all these things in January 2007 when my mother was diagnosed with terminal breast cancer. I remember so well the doctor coming into the waiting room and he looked at me with all the sadness in the world and said, 'Your mother needs you." At the time I did not realize the strongest woman I knew would deteriorate physically before my eyes within less than one year.

I entered her room and she sat with tears in her eyes and a look of shock and disbelief on her face. There was no need for words to be said I began to put the picture together. As we sat in the oncology office and my mother looked as if life had served her the final blow. She said, "I have cancer and there is no cure." It seemed that the breath was knocked out of my body but I was determined to fight this battle with her as long as she was willing.

Around April 2007 they started aggressive treatment of every kind, chemo was the worst. Every Wednesday she would come home weak and so very ill. She could barely make it to her bedroom. I remember getting up at 3am passing her cold wet towels and a pan to regurgitate in. There were days, and weeks she would go without eating. In less than 6 months she had lost over 100 pounds.

One evening I was in the kitchen preparing her lunch and she screamed for me. Upon entering her room I found her clutching the bed for dear life. She said the room was spinning and she felt like she was about to float off the bed. I then noticed the left side of her face was paralyzed and her left eye had no control as it was wondering back and forth. My first thought was she had a stroke. I drove her to the hospital because she hated being carried out of the house on a stretcher and neighbors would gather outside if they saw an ambulance in our yard. When we arrived to the hospital, the ER doctor explained she was experiencing vertigo and due to the cancer spreading to her brain she no longer had the use of the muscles located behind her left eye. I took her home that night and finally she cried but she also did something that angered me for well over 4 years…She prayed…She thanked God repeatedly, spoke in tongues, and fell on her knees and thanked God that things were as well as they were. I thought to myself she has no hair left, her nails are falling off due to treatments of various kinds, she is so little her clothes literally are falling off her, and now her left eye muscle is no longer strong enough to function but she is thanking God. I cannot explain the anger that filled my soul. For every word she cried in thanks I cried in disbelief. From that moment I decided I did not have a praise to give. I left her room and went as far as I could but one thing about God there is nowhere to run. I felt God had failed me again. First my Godmother passed away from a heart attack, then my Grandmother dies of old age, and now my best friend, my strong tower, my everything is dying before my eyes. I did everything I could to make my mother comfortable. We celebrated each holiday with smiles. She would never allowed us to feel sorry for her or treat her any different. She maintained her independence as long as she could. When she could no longer move about as she pleased, she still made her own appointments and paid bills by phone.

It wasn't until about February 2008 she lost her memory and began repeating herself. The doctors said there was no longer any need for cancer treatments and they placed her on hospice care. We moved in with my grandmother because deep down I could no longer handle the situation emotionally, physically, or spiritually.

After living with my grandmother for 2 weeks my mother was no longer laying in this hospital bed. The woman lying there was what was left after a lifetime of joy, happiness, pain, and determination. My mother helped everybody. She prayed and sang spirituals even after she had no mind to remember who I was. Two nights before she passed away my grandmother was bathing her and I heard them singing "Like the Dew in the Morning." It's amazing that she could no longer remember me but she had a spiritual connection that she could never forget.

On April 6th, 2008, she took her last breathe and went to be with the Lord. I had no thoughts in my heart of praising God for anything. I was angry (let me repeat that I was so angry) that the prayers, tears, and pleas we had all cried went unanswered. How could this all knowing, all powerful, all wise God allow this to happen. I became bitter and selfish. I began drinking and using drugs heavily. Now that I think back I did not do these things to ease my pain or help me through a rough times as many people say. I use alcohol, drugs, and men because it was the total opposite of my mother. I did not care who knew about my lifestyle. I wanted people to say, "She ain't nothing like her mother." Why, you may ask. I don't know I was angry and confused nothing made sense especially my behavior.

Now let me make this picture clear for you. I had a 4 year old son, a husband, brother, and sister. The obligation of being responsible for someone other than myself was even more exhausting than I care to acknowledge, so I didn't. My mother left us well taken care of and I spent money like it had no end. I partied and clubbed every time the doors opened. Many nights I walked out of the club when it was daybreak and slept until night fall. My son was raised by my mother and he was steadfast in praising God. Nightly he still had his own praise and worship service because this is what he and my mother practiced. I would drop him off at my aunts, grandmother, or cousin's house. I still went to church and I was great at going through the motions. I was raised in church so this task was easy. Many Sundays I went with a hangover to die from. When church let out I rushed home to find quiet so my head would stop spinning. If you notice I was clubbing and churching. I truly had no regard for pleasing God. If no clubs were open I would just start a party at my place. It was funny how liquor, music, and food will draw people and before I knew it there was a house full. One morning I remember waking up and the room was spinning I had no idea where my son was or who had him. The room was spinning and I experienced a true hangover I thought to myself Lord help me and a voice said "He don't care about you." At that moment anger once again fueled my rage and I turned up the Gin bottle beside my bed. I was always told to get over a hangover keep drinking what you drank the night before. So I indulged.

When you're on a downward spiral no one can stop you. It's not until you hit rock bottom you realize how far you've fallen. Life had passed me by days turn to weeks, weeks into months, Friday and Saturday partying had become everyday partying and hangovers turned into do-overs.

One night around 2am I was in what I refer to now as the devil's den. A place where you have let go of God's hand and embraced the devil's presence. I checked my cell phone and there was a text from my First Lady. When I saw her name I immediately sobered up and got up. All I remember reading was: "Daughter where art thou…"

I immediately left the house I was at and drove 90 miles an hour as if the devil truly was chasing me through the dark highway of Dauphin Island Parkway. I found an exit and pulled into a gas station, sat in my car, and cried for the first time. I did not cry for myself, I cried for my mother. All the effort she had put into raising me and I was out here chasing demons. I cried because I knew better but was not living better. I cried for my son who deserved better. I cried for my brother and sister who did not have the years I had with my mother. I cried for My God who had seen and heard me act like a fool and He still wanted me to know He loved me regardless of all I had done. My cell phone still in my hand I did not know what to say to My First Lady. I wondered did God show her what I was actually doing because she and God were real close. I just looked at the message and pulled away from the Chevron. I made it home and vowed to give my hurt, pained, and confused soul to God. I vowed to raise my son, love only my husband, and be a better example to my siblings.

This is where I made my Exodus. I began to look to the hills from which cometh my help. I gave God my hand and vowed never to turn back. Have I been perfect not by far, has everyday been sunshine, no it has not. Will I ever go back, not a chance! I have not fully accepted my calling but I strive every day to be better than the day before. No matter what comes my way I lean on God for understanding and I know His will is perfect and necessary. Everyone does not understand my praise just as I did not understand my mother's. However, in this life I've learned my break through is in my praise.

Broken Pieces

By: Itiah Lewis

Itiah Lewis
lewisitiah9@gmail.com

I remember sitting and thinking should I write my story or do I really want my story to be told. I was so nervous for numerous reasons, one being embarrassed knowing my family and friends will be reading what I have been through and all my obstacles I had to overcome; two being judged and people saying, "She's so dumb. She deserved it!" Not everyone understands or is compassionate to stories like mine. However, my biggest concern was the person I wrote about reading it. So much emotion was going through my head and still is. The past feelings rushed me and I was angry all over again. I prayed to God to provide me with guidance and he did just that.

It was clear to me that it's my time to let my story be known. I wanted to help any other woman that can relate to my story heal while going through her own. I realized that I had to start thinking for myself and not care what people thought of me or how they would react.

I always wanted to be an author and a motivational speaker. I love writing about mysteries but I never imagined writing the most private portions of my life for the world to read. I didn't want to talk about my own story, about my abuse, but it was time to do so.

I will continue to follow my dreams and keep my faith in God and allow my stories to be told. I'm a Catalina like the flower blossoming into Growth, Conquering and Grace. Fate might have dealt me this hand of cards but I will choose how I play them. I encourage you to take the hand that you have been dealt and play it to your advantage.

As a woman we find ourselves being available for everyone else. We are that shoulder to cry on, that encourager, that friend. But who do we turn to when we need all of those things?

Often times when we have the turbulence in our lives we turn to what is comfortable. When we've painted ourselves into that fictitious corner we turn to what we know. Sometimes that familiar thing is the opposite sex. We turn to a man for fulfillment and to love anticipating its reciprocation.

When I was 17 years old, I was in an abusive relationship. The turmoil has changed my life forever. It changed my whole outlook on life. I'm very antisocial and I suffer from a lot of anxiety. I'm not a people person anymore and I just lost all faith and hope in humanity. I tried counseling and talking to my pastor. It helped a little bit but I quickly realized that in order for me to move on from all the hurt I had to forgive. I would never forget the terror I went through and had to overcome. I know you're reading this and you're likely saying to yourself, "how could she put herself through this at 17?" You're probably wondering where my parents were. I don't have a story like many, my parents were always there for me. I came from a good home. I just was very rebellious. I wanted to do things my way, I ignored all the things my parents taught me. I wanted to live life as I saw fit, however, I didn't know how close I was to not living at all.

I remember it just like it was yesterday. I met him around the 4th of July. I was 17 and he was 27. I was walking home from the rain station in Queens. He was driving a black escalade with 24inch rims. Because I was young that immediately caught my attention. He followed me all the way home honking his horn and trying to talk to me. I ignored him until I got in front of my house, for some reason that made me safe. He got out of the truck and immediately I noticed his light brown eyes and his smooth caramel complexion. He had on a fitted cap and his braids hung down his back. He was like nothing that I had ever seen. He was a fresh breathe of air.

At 17 I was inexperienced. I had never been intimate with a man but his very presence enticed me. I wanted to be with him in a sexual way, even though that was foreign to me. Something about him kept me smiling and intrigued, maybe it was that Brooklyn game he was talking.

This man was so persistent. He charmed me with his ability to financially sustain me. He wanted me to go to Disney and meet his parents in Dayton, Ohio. I was reluctant but he begged and begged until I agreed. I decided that I'd better bring my god-sister just to be safe, he agreed. I lied to my parents and told them that I would be staying with my cousin on the other side of town. I didn't even pack a bag, he bought everything for me once we hit Orlando. On the way to Orlando we drove to Ohio to pick up his parents. We had so much fun. It was beyond amazing. However, all great things must come to an end. During the second week of out stay he slapped me. I was shocked because it was not warranted and it was with such force I literally saw starts. The only thing that I could do was run. I ran out of the room. I had no idea where I was going, but I knew that I had to get away from him. He chased me down and he apologized. I forgave him. That day changed my life forever. I knew in my heart I should not have trusted him but of course me being young and unwise I stayed with him knowing what he was capable of.

After returning to Brooklyn I decided to be honest with my parents. I told them the truth. To say that they were disappointed was an understatement. I introduced my parent to my new love and he asked my parents if he could fly me back to Orlando in 2 weeks. He said that he had a surprise for me, they said yes.

Upon my arrival in Orlando, to my surprise he booked a 5 star hotel. The room was beautiful and had a bottle of wine, chilled and waiting for us. I walked in our hotel room and he asked me to marry him and I said yes of course. It seemed that as soon as I said yes his position in my life and the expectation that he had for me changed. He asked, "Are you ready to have sex?" I said, "No." I guess my response was unacceptable because he took it from me and said he owned me now and no one could do anything about it. I was so scared. I could not tell my parents any of this.

After being on our adventure in Orlando he took me to Kissimmee. To my surprise he has bought a house and expected me to live there with him. I was so amazed. Although I was amazed I was afraid. I knew that I needed to go home to my parents, I didn't though. I was so deep in love with this man I couldn't leave his side. For a year we were happy. Shortly after our year of being there the beatings started again. I remember one night I came home around 10 pm. I had been on a date with my best friend Quinton. We went to dinner and a movie. By the time I got home he was waiting by the door with a belt. I was 5 months pregnant at the time. He explained that he wasn't mad that I was out with my best friend, because he was gay and not a threat. He was angry because I home at 10 and didn't like the fact I was having so much fun. He beat me so badly and threw me down the stairs. I began to bleed, he took me to the hospital and they advised me that I had a miscarriage. I could have told but I was too scared to say anything. He beat me for years and sometimes he would punished me by raping me anally. He wouldn't stop until I apologized and he felt that it was sincere. After he raped me he made me snort cocaine or take Xanax to mask the pain. If I refused he would beat me again.

After the beating stopped a gift would appear outside of my bedroom door. He would send me a text letting me know that I could them. I was always locked in a room unless I was behaving or his family was in town. I was so brainwashed that he had me believing that I had no one that loved me but him. I believed every word he told me.

Eventually I reached my breaking point. The beatings and the gifts kept coming. I finally got the coverage to leave him. I remember that it was 5 am. He went to take Cocaine, our white red nosed pit bull for a walk, I left everything behind, my clothes, and my green Honda accord that my mom gave me. I took my ring off my finger and left it on the pillow, I gathered the money he always gave me that I had been saving. I walked to the corner and caught a cab to the bus station. He finally noticed I was gone and it seemed he knew just where to find me. He arrived as I awaited the arrival of the bus. He came there threatening and begging me to stay. He asked if he could talk to me and I agreed.

When we left that bus station I didn't know what I was going to walk into. I didn't know that he was had already planned my murder. He had borrowed a gun from a friend and he tied me up. There was plastic was everywhere. I knew what he was going to do. I told him, "if you're going to kill me at least tell my parents that you did it or let them know where my body at so they can bury me correctly." He made me beg him not to kill me. I wept and urinated on myself. Eventually, he let me go because I promised him I would not leave him.

The next morning he told me that he trusted me and to show me he was going to take me to visit my mother who was in Miami. Miami afforded me a great opportunity, space and time. As soon as we arrived I disappeared. Until this day he has yet to find me physically. He has attempted to contact me on Facebook, apologizing to me. I didn't want to hear it because I recognize now that if you loved then you wouldn't have hurt me. How could you beat me and take me away from my family? That couldn't be love.

I finally saw his pictures. It appears that he has a whole new family. Sometimes I wonder if his wife knows his deep dark secrets. I wonder if she knows that he has the potential to hurt her like he did me.

I pray that whoever reads this will never experience what I've been through and if you are in this situation please reach out to someone or leave. Please know that it's not worth your life. I have no regrets for leaving. Today, I have a great husband and wonderful children. If I had stayed I would not have made it and I am convinced of that. In this time, I give my all to GOD, he is my savior. He saved my life and I am able to tell my story today because of that fact.

My Paradox

By: C.J. Lane

How can you be the victim of a crime and still the one at fault?
How can a secret still be a secret if you tell everyone you know?
How can someone too weak to hold a child carry the burdens of a man?
It's too confusing to comprehend?
Step into my paradox...

How can I be over something that I think about every day?
Cry dry tears that stream down my face.
Can't show too much real emotion,
Might get figured out.
Step into my paradox...

Helping everyone else
To prevent helping my self
It's a trick no one sees but me
Like children playing hide and go seek
Step into my paradox...

The only place where you can find me
Is in these words I speak my peace
Verbs and nouns, brain and soul meet
Around the bend here we go again
Step into my paradox...

I know its past time for me to let it go
And I'm trying to everyday
But I've got to do it in my way

Travel with me or stay behind
Step into my paradox…

Am I a good girl or am I bad
Feel my feelings happy or sad
A smile on my face doesn't mean I'm glad
A bout of laughter might mean I'm mad.
Step into my paradox…

A winding road under a rickety bridge
Slippery slope and I have slid.
A bumpy path with a fork in the road
Navigation on Spanish mode
Step into my paradox…

Am I up or am I down
A brand new queen with a broken crown
I want this feeling to go away
I want to leave but I have to stay
Step into my paradox…

I'm getting it out the best way I know how
I'm putting pen to pad writing this thing down
Because I'm not trying to hold on
I want to be free
Breaking out of my paradox…

Happy Anniversary

By: Jeanette Benjamin

Jeanette Benjamin
AUTHOR OF
ISABELLA GOES TO HAITI

jpepinb58@aol.com
www.fttrworldoutreach.com

When Xaviera told me about the Exodus Project, I thought this would be a great idea. Sharing the input of women's experiences from their lives into a book that would definitely help so many woman would be a divine blessing. Then she asked me to participate, I was overcome with emotions. There are so many things that cause us pain in our lives and choosing one would be hard.

I chose the one that had the greatest impact in my life. Although at the time I did not know why I was going through this but then I realized that sometimes we go through the fire in order to help someone along the way, which I have.

I sat with the thought of returning to school and for the life of me I couldn't muster up the desire to return. I pondered this decision long and hard, finally I spoke with my husband Jack. Jack already had an Associate's degree and he wanted to continue his education to obtain a Bachelors in Social Work. Now, I thought it would be better for him to go because he had the desire and because it was free. What I didn't calculate was the fact that this would mean that our household income would drastically reduce.

To compensate for the financial blow we suffered I picked up lots of extra hours. Although the hours were long and the work was hard I did it with joy. It made me feel so good to know that I was doing this for my family. I was making this sacrifice for my husband. Even though at the time I did not feel so appreciated for my efforts it did not matter. I started to think of other ways to generate more income. He was in school full time so the responsibility definitely fell in my lap. As fate would have it I met an individual that became a really good friend. She and I decided to get involved in property renovations and management. Jack was so hesitant because she was homosexual. However, after a while he saw that I was very persistent and he agreed. Within the first year we purchased six properties. My time became very limited because I was working full-time and I was working long hours at the properties.

I could see the financial strides that we were making but the more successful in business I was the worse my marriage became. My marriage was suffocating and I couldn't figure it out. Like most men Jack was not an effective communicator. I didn't know where the disconnect was occurring because he wasn't talking to me about it.

Although my marriage was heading south at least I had my business. At least that's what I thought. As the second year approached things became hectic within my business relationship. I knew that we would have to part ways when I had to punch her in the face. I felt so bad but that was the moment that I realized that there was something wrong with me.

I've never been in a place that it seemed that I was searching for something that I didn't even know that I had lost. I was so disconnected, so detached from everything. I stopped going to church and I didn't have enough strength to even pray. I couldn't keep up the charade, the pretending day in and day out. My children were in their late teens and early twenties so I know that they recognized that something was wrong.

I can recall my 25th wedding anniversary approaching, I never had a formal wedding and wanted one. I was 17 when I got married so a wedding wasn't really a priority. I talked to Jack about it and he agreed. I was so excited putting this all together as I had never planned a wedding. I purchased a beautiful ivory wedding dress, I was in seventh heaven. However, months prior to wedding my husband really started changing. His attitude was horrible, he was hanging with some retired military friends, and he was staying out until 4am with no explanation.

I began having some serious anxiety attacks and fell into a deep depression. Because of the added stressors in my marriage I started having panic attacks. These attacks were so severe that I was admitted into the ER several times. I was prescribed psychotropic medication from my counselor that I had been seeing a year prior but it didn't seem to help. I didn't have the support that I craved from my husband. He believed that I was the problem and the only thing that needed to be fixed in our marriage was me. He refused to participate in therapy and I felt abandoned.

The excitement of the wedding was wearing very thin. However, it was too late to call off the wedding because many invites were coming from out of state including my precious father. When my father and sisters along with my niece arrived a few days before the wedding I felt relieved. I felt that I was surrounded by people who loved and cared about me. I felt that this was a great time to take my father to Disney. Although he was 82 he was a man filled with life and spirit. I recall getting on Space Mountain, we were all securely in our seats. As the ride started and terror overwhelmed me I realized that if I was this terrified that my 82 year old father who had a pacemaker had to have succumbed to the trauma.

As I climbed out of the ride I sat in my numbness awaiting the delivery of the news that my wedding had instantly turned into a funeral. To my surprise he walked out with his hat and trench coat in place. He was okay and that was the assurance that I needed. We laughed as he told us that we had plotted to kill him.

The night before the wedding I ended up sleeping on the sofa. I kept thinking what a mistake I was making. I was so upset. The wedding itself was beautiful about 60 people were in attendance and I enjoyed my father and sisters company. When I walked down the aisle I wanted my husband to look at me like the men that I've seen in the wedding reality shows. They look at their bride to be with eyes that look right inside her and their feelings become one. They even get teary eyed. I didn't get that. I got a man looking at me like, let's get this over with. After the wedding we headed home, my husband changed clothes and left me at home, alone. He did not return until the next morning. I was glad my father and sisters were leaving the next day because I could not keep up the simulation of this "happy marriage".

I was falling deeper and deeper into a depression. I thought that the wedding would bring us closer but it didn't. Living like this was horrible. I could not eat or sleep but yet I had to maintain my home and work full time.

By now Jack had graduated from school and he was in the process of searching for employment but he would stay out for hours without an explanation or regard for my feelings. One particular day after getting home close to bed time I decided to get some answers. As he made his way to the kitchen I looked in his coat pocket and found a picture of another woman. I went crazy. I was crying hysterically. I could not control myself and of course my husband said nothing.

The next day I did not go to work, I stayed home and started sorting out my important documents. I even called my insurance company and asked them if a person committed suicide would the insurance pay out, they said yes. That was the assurance that I needed. I called my business partner and told her I would get together all of the business paperwork. She felt that was odd and called my counselor who then called me. I cannot remember what I said to her but by that evening I had a call from someone at the Sheriff's Dept. He kept me on the phone for a while, a very long while. I was shocked when my husband came into the bedroom and said to me, "you don't know what you have done." I was stunned. I did not know what he was talking about. A deputy had come to the house with a suicide prevention team, I was baker acted on the spot. I was so embarrassed.

While in this horrible place, after 3 days the psychiatrist requested Jack to have a meeting. I will never forget that day he showed up all dressed up. It was Valentine's Day and he had nothing for me. The doctor asked him if he felt I should go home, my husband said NO. I should stay there for a while longer.

I wanted to jump over the desk and attack this man, but I guess I was in too much shock to even move. I went back to my room really wanting to die. I think that I even felt that a part of me had died in the meeting. The next day one of the male techs said he wanted to talk to me, he was my help. He started telling me how I am worth more than I was giving myself credit. He said I did not need a man to tell me what I was worth. Those words penetrated my spirit. I got myself on track. After that talk I reached out for the Lord I had put aside. I reached out to him as if it was the first time I had known him. When I was released I started going to church and even asked for prayers. Things started changing within me. I had no idea why I felt that I should tolerate a person who did not encourage me or see my pain.

In all of this I realized that Jesus is our one and only crutch. He is the one we should seek approval from. The one who fills our heart with the utmost joy. When we find ourselves in a dark hole it is best not to look within ourselves but to look up to the light.

Reflecting on this dark time I realized that as we get older changes occur and so does our relationship with our spouses. You either grow together or grow apart. Some men tend to lock themselves in a bubble not looking or realizing that the wife is hurting. They look at it as, "there goes that emotional woman."

Being in the hospital opened my eyes to knowing I am in charge of me, no one has the right to put me down or make me feel less than who I am. I have learned that the Lord is in control and the focus should be on him, even if your marriage is not the fairytale you wanted it to be, the Lord is your Knight in Shining Armor.

If They Say So

By: LaToya Perry

LaToya Perry

OWNER OF BIG, BOLD, AND BEAUTIFUL

latoyamooreperry@gmail.com

When I first heard about the Exodus Project I knew I wanted to be a part of it. I wanted to be able to tell you how you are not the only person that feels neglected. I wanted to be able to connect with you so that you know that you are not alone. I knew this project would not only help you but me as well. As I have been through so much in my lifetime I had to decide which event in my life I wanted to share.

I chose this particular one because I felt as if there are a lot of people who needed to read it. We all go through some trying times and wish that we could make them go away. I wanted to be able to help you get through this as I have. Sometimes when we feel alone and forget in the process how strong we really are. I wanted to make sure you remember that you are the strongest person you know. You can overcome any and everything that you put your mind to. Always let yourself know that you are smart, strong, and wise. No problem is too big to solve.

When I was growing up I made a lot of bad choices. I was really smart and enjoyed doing a lot of things. I was even on a cheerleading squad that actually made it to the national cheerleading competition. I can remember it like it was yesterday, standing in a packed room full of cheering fans and other squads. The screams and cheers filled my body with excitement. I was ten years old and it was the very first cheerleading competition that I had attended. My thoughts raced and in that moment I believed that I could do anything. When they announced the winners I could feel my heart drop to the bottom of my stomach. We came in third place in the competition but we rejoiced as if we had won first place. The ride home was so much fun. We knew we were good but we did not expect to place third. We were just happy that we were given a chance to be a part of the competition. It was nice to be able to feel like I was a part of something amazing.

Shortly after placing in the national competition things at the recreation center began to change and we were no longer spending as much time there. Cheerleading was my escape. It made me come alive and now I had to find new ways to occupy my time. As I began to search for other things that gave me the same feeling I started to rebel against my mother. I was talking back and acting out. Although I was being disrespectful at home I still managed to make good grades in school.

When I turned 14 years old I began to hang out with some of my older cousins. What I didn't realize is that with an older crowd came older things that I wasn't equipped to handle. I started going to parties and missing curfew. I felt as if I could get away with anything and I was really trying my luck. My mother had to put me on punishment every other day because I was not listening to her. The more I hung out with my cousins the more they introduced me to sex. I began kissing guys and letting them touch me inappropriately. These things made me curious about sex. I asked my cousins all types of questions because they were already sexually active and had babies. I was so sure that I would not be like them. I felt comfortable experimenting with sex because I knew I was a bit more mature. I actually thought that I had this thing down to a science.

The guy that I decided to experience sex with was older than me but he was a virgin as well. We had no clue what we were doing. I liked the fact that my first time was with someone who was not experienced just like me. This guy made me feel safe. He took his time with me and handled me with care. I just knew he was going to be the one. Shortly after we began having sex I found out that he was interested in more than just me. He violated every ounce of trust that I had for him when I learned that he was trying to pursue one of my friends. I thought this person cared about me but I was wrong.

I learned quickly that becoming sexually active was a mistake. It seemed as if it was a snowball effect. I started having sex with people I didn't really care about or know for that matter. I was sneaking around to be with guys who only wanted me to have sex with them. My mother even caught a guy at our house. Even though we were not having sex that day I still felt the need to hide him. When she came into my room she went straight to the closet where he was hiding. I thought maybe I should have told him to get into the tub. Yeah right who am I kidding she would have still found him. I still do not know what made her come home early that day. That did not stop me though.

It took my adulthood to show me that I was having sex to fill the void of needing to feel wanted. Several months later I became acquainted with a guy that was 4 years older than I. We decided to exclusively see each other. What I thought was wonderful was the biggest mistake. This relationship was the worst one ever. My self-esteem was so low that I let this guy walk all over me. I accepted the fact that he was cheating on me and that he only wanted me for my body. From the results of feeling unloved and unwanted I allowed this guy to have his way with me. Even though we were using condoms I still somehow became pregnant with my first child. In my mind I thought, "I'm 15 years old, in the 9th grade, and about to have a baby. What am I going to do?" I tried to hide my pregnancy as long as I could because I was afraid to tell my mother. For some reason the more I tried to hide it the more sick I became. I don't think I ever in my life have thrown up as much as I did during this time. I believe my mom began to suspect something was wrong because out of the blue she decided that she wanted to take me to the free clinic and put me on birth control. When she told me she had set the appointment for me and my sister to go, my heart dropped. I already knew what the results were going to be. I can remember thinking, "Once I go to this place it will make everything official".

The appointment was set for the next day and my mother called my cousin so that she could take my sister and me. As my cousins pulled up to the clinic my heart began to pound as if it was trying to jump out of my chest. When the nurse called me to the back my legs felt numb and I could not move. I was just that nervous. I already knew what she was going to tell me. I went into the bathroom to take the pregnancy test and when the nurse read the results, I remember crying so hard that my entire face was red and my eyes were puffy. The nurse looked as if she wanted to cry with me. All I could think about was how my mom was going to react.

As I was leaving the clinic with my little brown bag I was hoping nobody would ask me what was in it. Of course, my sister, being the pain in the ass she is snatched my bag and looked inside. She laughed as if it was funny, and said, "I can't wait to get home so I can tell mama."

As we slowly approached our house I took my time to walk in. The first thing my mom said, even before my sister could open her big mouth was, "So what did they say? I know you are pregnant." I just held my head down. She told me that I was going to be the one that had to tell my stepfather. My stepfather treated me as if I was his own. I did not want to disappoint him. When I walked into the room where he was, it took me a while to get it out. Once I told him, the look he gave me made me feel as if he was so hurt and disappointed by my bad choices. Just by looking at him I could feel the pain in his heart. He did not speak to me for a long time. We would pass each other in the house as if we were strangers.

I had to have the dreaded discussion with my mom about who the father was but I did not want to tell her. My mom took me to my cousin's house where I was always hanging out and she asked them if they knew who the father of my baby was. One of my cousin's did not hesitate to tell all. She gave names and addresses; I was outraged. To my surprise my biological father came arrived. As I poured my heart poured my heart out he grew more and more disappointed. I can remember his exact words, "How can you be pregnant? Now you will never finish school. You will never be able to follow your dreams. I thought you were better than this. I do not blame you I blame your mother." Those words really touched me. After he said those things to me, I realized I had to show him that just because I was having a baby, it does not mean my life is over.

After having my baby I fell behind in my classes which led me to attend alternative school so I could make up my credits. I was there for one school year and was able to get caught up so I could return to regular school my junior year. When returning to school I met this guy who I fell completely in love with. I knew I loved him when I couldn't think of anyone else but him. We talked on the phone for hours every single day. We started hanging out after school. I introduced him to my baby and he still stuck around.

After some time our relationship turned sexual. Although we generally used condoms, one day we didn't. That one day changed my life and his. I got pregnant with my second child. I thought having one baby was tough but I knew that being a teen mother of two was incredibly hard. I began to hear all types of things from everywhere and everybody. They said, "Look at her she will never graduate." They said, "She cannot do anything but have kids." They said, "She will always live off the government." They said, "She will never go to college." Those were all of the things that were being said about me. I felt as if my life was the topic of everybody's discussion and no matter how hard I worked it was never good enough.

By the time I graduated from high school I was a mother of two. I walked across that stage so very proud of myself because nobody thought I could do it. They even said, "The only reason she graduated was because she was dating the principal's son." I wondered why I was always the topic of discussion. I was determined to graduate high school regardless of what everybody was saying about me. I knew my potential and no matter how much they tried to take it away from me I was not letting them. I worked hard to get my diploma and nobody cared. It was as if I just existed for them to have something to say.

After graduation I decided that it was time for me and my children to have a place of our own, a home. The day I signed my lease for my first apartment was one of the happiest days of my life. When I moved into my place it felt too good to be true. I did not have to follow anyone else rules or hear any complaints. After everything that I had been through I became stronger and stronger. I was determined to be self-sufficient and independent for me and my children. I didn't want to be a burden and I didn't want a crutch. Sometimes I felt as if we were a burden and nobody wanted to be bothered with us. I made it a personal goal of mine to make successfulness a priority. It was really hard but I was determined.

I struggled a lot but we made it work. Although we were surviving it didn't erase the thoughts of what others had said. I started to believe that all I could do was make babies, at least that's what they said. I guess getting pregnant a third time didn't help the situation at all. I was so ashamed. My second child was only five months old and here I am pregnant again. I quit college because of complications with the pregnancy. The talking started again of course. They said, "I told you that you were not going to be able to go to college. I told you that it would not work. Why are you trying to work and go to school with two babies and one on the way? That's impossible."

That was such a very low point for me. But one thing that I learned in those lonely moments was if we let what other people say stop us from achieving our goals we will become the person that they are attempting to create. It took me a while but I eventually got back into school. I was a fulltime college student with three kids and a fulltime job. Having three babies, working fulltime, and school fulltime was so difficult but we made it work. I felt as if I was never going to accomplish my other goals. The thing that was the hardest was finding someone to babysit my kids while I worked and went to school. I remember thinking, "Why is it so hard for me to find somebody to watch my kids so that I could better myself. It's a lot of girls my age that have no problem getting a babysitter and they are in the club every weekend."

Since finding a babysitter was such a difficult task in order to make it work for us I started taking online classes. That way we wouldn't need a babysitter. I wanted to prove everybody wrong. I knew I was destined for greatness even if they didn't. Sometimes we have to motivate ourselves when others doubt us. My biggest motivation and drive came from me wanting to show everybody that they were wrong about me. I made it my mission to show them how smart I was. It took me a while to get everything together but I graduated college with a degree in Accounting. Upon completion I started to set more goals for myself. You have to set goals and when you reach them set more goals. It was hard for me to achieve the things that I wanted to achieve especially with people constantly telling me that I couldn't. After hearing you can't for so long you begin to think what they think. You have to remain focused on your hopes and dreams because only you can make them happen. I know it may have taken me a long time to achieve some of my goals but once I accomplished my goal it was the best feeling in the world.

I just want you to know that just because you make a few mistakes it does not mean your life is over. When I graduated from college the second time I actually attended the commencement ceremony. I can honestly say I felt more proud of myself than I ever had before. When I put that cap and gown on I knew there was a brighter future ahead of me. It felt great to have people cheer for me for completing one of my goals. I was able to share my day with my little sister and that just made it all worth the wait. Now that there will always be naysayers but look at me, now a mother of five, two time college graduate, and making a good living for myself. You would think people would be happy for me but instead they are now saying, "Oh she doesn't have a Bachelor's Degree." I worked really hard to get to where I am and it took me a long time to realize that what other people think about me is irrelevant. Because I love myself. I still have a lot of goals to complete and no matter what happens I will complete them. Just remember you can do anything you want to do regardless of what other people think. As long as you work hard and have faith it can be done.

Keeping Secrets and Telling Lies

By: Neema Campbell

Neema Campbell

Neema.Campbell@live.com

When I was presented with the opportunity to be a part of such an awesome movement, I was immediately excited. That excitement slowly turned into a form of anxiety. Did I really want to bleed on pages to women I didn't know? Would my story actually help someone?

I can say that being able to talk to someone, or hear a testimony of what it is like to overcome a situation made me feel stronger. This took me back to a scripture in Revelation that said that we all overcome by our testimonies.

I pray that you read these few pages of my life, and learn and grow. I pray that you find a story of strength, and the power of overcoming. Know that the pit is only deep until you decide to take the first step and do the work it takes to get back on the road to recovery.

I have been a secret keeper and a story teller for as long as I can remember. I have always been the one that people can rely on to keep everything so quiet that when it does finally come out, people are like "you knew and didn't tell me?" I could also alter my reality by coming up with one that was more exciting than the one I currently lived in. Often I would hear "that girl knows she can lie. I mean who can tell a story like that without blinking?" My secret life has always been protected by barbed wire. It was top security, booby trapped, and Fort Knox all tied in to one. I always thought that keeping secrets was a great quality to have until I was fourteen years old going to the ER with an ulcer, and suffering from panic attacks. It turns out that those secrets were more like poison killing me slowly from the inside. I never knew that my storytelling was also a mechanism used to block out my reality in order to create my own. I grew tired of the life I had at an early age, but didn't know why it was so much easier to "go away" and create what I wanted. Later, I would find out this was known as disassociation.

At 35, I sit back and wonder where the start of my secret keeper days came from. Was I just wired this way? Did holding on to stories, and actions of others make me feel inferior to them? Was this just a way of saying I didn't trust anyone? Because I began to start soul searching in my thirties, I decided to really dive in and seek out some truth about myself. I started my search on my knees. I figured the only way to truly get to know who I was destined to be was to go to the One

Who created me. Take this note from me, if you aren't ready for God to reveal who you are to you, do not ask Him. When I asked, He surely had no problem answering. I am still getting answers today from questions I asked years ago.

I was six years old when my innocence was taken in a closet from an older cousin. He asked me if I wanted to see something special then told me I could only see it in the closet. My cousin exposed himself and made me perform oral sex. Then he released himself and told me to swallow all that he put in my mouth. His brother then came and did the same thing. Later, they took turns touching all over my body and kept asking how it felt. I went into that closet an innocent little girl; I left a broken, confused shell of a little girl. I had no idea what just happened to me. I sat there with a mouth full of sticky stuff, and I felt dirty. I don't know why I felt dirty. I guess somewhere in me just knew that what happened shouldn't have.

They both left me in the closet when they were finished. It took me a while to come out and back into the bedroom. They told me that if I ever told anyone that I would not be believed, so I had better keep my mouth shut. I didn't say a word for two years.

I was at the dinner table with my family for Sunday dinner. I was so full that I just blurted out "they touched me in the closet when I was six" as if I was as if I was asking someone to pass me the dinner rolls. I didn't even mention what else happened because I couldn't muster up the strength to repeat it. Even though I had this experience years ago, it felt like it just happened yesterday. My family paused stunned that I just said that as casual as the Sunday dinner we just started eating. My father asked me "Why didn't you tell us sooner?" I responded with my head down and shrugged my shoulders. He responded "well, there is nothing we can do about it now." Dinner continued as if I never said a word. It was that very moment I vowed never to speak on anything again. The seed of the secret keeper had been planted in the closet; the response from my family fertilized it and helped it grow.

At the age of nine, the cycle repeated itself with another male cousin. This time it lasted for years. At the time he was fourteen, and seemed to be one of my coolest cousins ever. We often played games, and I always thought he gave me a lot of attention. That meant a lot to a little girl who felt invisible at the time. There was this one time that he came to visit from out of town with some other family. We all had a really good time with swimming, laughing and playing, and just enjoying family time. That night while everyone was asleep, he woke me up to tell me that he wanted me to lie close to him so we could talk before he fell asleep. Because I heard this tone in a male's voice before I had my suspicions, but went over to him anyway. When I got next to him, he began to caress my body as if I were no longer his little cousin, but rather a teenage girl who was interested in becoming his girlfriend. He told me that he felt I was special, and that he would teach me how to please a man. This way every time I would see him, he wouldn't have to keep teaching me because I would already know what I was doing. That night I learned how to fondle a man and massage his body until he had an orgasm. I finally found out what the sticky stuff was years ago that was released in my mouth while in that closet many years ago. The next morning I again heard that no one would believe me if I told, and even if I did tell they would all be mad at me. Based off of the previous response I figured no one would care. So I kept my mouth shut for years. Every time we saw one another I was being touched, or grabbed, or grabbed him in some sort of way. There was always a game of "house" where I was the mom and he was the dad. I always had to make sure the dad was satisfied because he would say "that is what good moms did in the real world" I was told. As months turned in to years, he grew tired of only touching. When I was around twelve, he tried to penetrate me. With just sticking the tip of him inside of me I felt a pain I had never felt before. I screamed so loudly that it forced him to stop. He never asked if I was ok, he simply got up fixed his clothes, reminded me to be quiet because I had family upstairs, and walked away. He told me he will have to stretch me out so that I can be able to take him inside of me the way a girlfriend should. Five years had gone by with my being touched, kissed, grinded on, and partially penetrated by him.

At 14, the time with my cousin was finally over. Not because I told someone and they listened. It was over because he said he found another girlfriend who could handle him. Part of me was heartbroken because I felt a break up. Somehow in my mind I became okay with the fact that my cousin claimed me as his girlfriend. I felt wanted and loved by someone. I didn't like that I had to do to get the love, but I enjoyed what I thought was love and attention at that time. Whenever he and I had our encounters, I would drift off in my mind. My body would be getting touched and I could mentally not feel it any longer. When I drifted off, I could get up from what just happened without feeling like I wanted to die. Sometimes if I drifted far enough, I wouldn't even think about it for a couple of days.

Even after it was done, I never spoke of us. I just tucked my experiences, and feelings deep on the inside of me. Realizing my secrets were making me sick, I learned to start self-medicating with marijuana, drinking, and rebellious behavior. These highs took me further than any drifting off could. There were a lot more stoned, drunk days than sober. Looking back I realized it was nothing but the Lord Himself that kept me from becoming a full blown addict.

As the years passed, my parents went through one of what I deem the worst divorces ever at that time as well. Being the youngest of three, I was the only one in the house when the proceedings began. At this time I still hadn't said a word of what happened for all those years with my cousin. I never brought it up to him because I felt if I did, nothing would happen. I was angry, but had no idea how to express that at the time. I opted to simply smile and act as if nothing was wrong.

Meanwhile, I started going through major mood swings. I could go from feeling so euphoric that I could conquer the entire world, to being so depressed I couldn't move. This would happen within hours of the same day. With all of this inner turmoil, I still had to go to school. I remember walking the halls of my school knowing that people had no idea how I felt, and what I was dealing with was more important than algebraic equations. Mixing drugs and drinking with these feelings led to a day where I attempted to take my own life by cutting my wrists. I don't even remember feeling any pain. I didn't expect to wake up the next morning, but I did. I went to school that day and told my school nurse "last night I tried to slit my wrists" as if I were telling her I had a headache. Telling her this led to a three day stint in a mental hospital designed for teens.

When I first got there, I was spooked for real. There were kids in there talking to shadows, and telling me that people were sitting in chairs that weren't there. I couldn't have any sharp objects in my possession, they took my shoe strings, and the windows had bars on them.

My parents looked so shocked that their youngest baby was in a mental hospital. Their eyes looked so confused. It amazed me then how people can't see, even when it is right in front of them. They didn't see my pain, they didn't my struggle. Even in the hospital, I just felt that if they didn't see me in the fragile state I was in, they would never see me.

Daily I had group therapy sessions where we would go around in a circle talking about our feelings. Journaling also became a way of releasing for me. I remember writing for hours. The more I would write the less heavy I began to feel.

While in the hospital I was diagnosed with bipolar disorder. Personal therapy sessions, and medicine began to help me get stabilized in how I felt each day. After three days, I was released to go home as long as I continued much needed therapy.

Once I was out of the hospital, I got back into the daily regime of going to school, and I even got a job. Although I made sure I wrote in my journal, and went to therapy, there was still so much anger and pain that I didn't deal with quite yet. Thankfully, I still graduated on time from high school. Talk about a miracle! I truly believe all of those prayers my family prayed had a lot to do with that.

I come from a family with a strong religious background and I was taught early about the power of prayer. "God always hears you," my grandma would say. I wanted to believe her, but I just couldn't fathom how the God who loves me would let all of these terrible things happen to me so early in life. I would be at church every Sunday, and even sung in the choir, but I didn't know who God was and if he was indeed for me. I had always felt He like everyone else who was supposed to protect me had left me to fend for myself. I was at a noon day prayer service I remember telling God, "If you are indeed real and have been here this whole time, show me." To show me that He heard my hearts cry, that very day He saved me. From that day, I have been getting my heart healed one day at a time.

One of the biggest parts of healing is the power of forgiveness. Learning this was one of the hardest things for me to do because I felt as if forgiveness was the same as saying that being molested, raped, mistreated, and ignored was ok. Even after salvation, I felt I had the right to hold them prisoner. One by one they had to be forgiven. This was the only way my life could be what I wanted it to be. I had to release the people, the secrets, and the pain. With much time, much prayer, sleepless nights, and many tears the forgiveness process began.

One year during Thanksgiving, my father and I began having a conversation about parenthood. As an adult, I still wanted an answer to why he responded the way he did at the dinner table when I was younger. He looked at me, and with concern he said "Neema, I am so sorry. I should have done better." The little girl in me needed that. The grown woman in me wanted to experience love from her dad. That day, I got it. That released me to release him.

While it was hard to forgive others, it was even harder to forgive myself. I was convinced that I was at fault not only for the things that happened to me, but the choices I made that lead to such a tumultuous life. There were so many days I wanted to fight for a better change in my life, and learn to produce a better way of thinking. Once you have allowed yourself to become a victim, and embrace a negative thought process, it can be extremely tedious to change. However, it is not impossible.

Every day, I had to make the decision to forgive myself and that I deserved to have the life that God intended for me. There were days I was all for the changing process, and then there were days I felt as if it was all for naught. These were the days I had to keep making the step towards my goals. Especially the days I didn't feel like it.

With many years that have passed, and now as a mom of two daughters of my own I realize that the little girl I was those years ago is living in both of them. They have motivated me to keep living to obtain my best me. They helped me realize that through it all I am still standing and God is showing who He is in my life day by day as long as I take the step.

The more I begin to release inner thoughts and secrets on the inside of me through honesty in writing, the less I had to "drift" away into another life because the one I was living was unbearable. Every day I chose to live my real life, it gets better. Every day I choose to see myself as my Father sees me; I am one step closer to my destiny. Every day that I choose to be honest with who I am a deeper level of healing takes place.

These choices ensure that my little girls don't have to have the same story I had as a little girl. These choices help me to grow stronger every day. These choices are a testimony that I can share with the little girls of the world. It is my prayer that my testimony will inspire someone else to come out of the closet, forgive, and learn to love and live as God intended.

The Spirit of Sabotage
By: Minister Rose Shaw

Minister Rose Shaw
shawmountvernon@aol.com

I am the voice of the millions of women who find themselves hiding out in the masses. Women that have been broken, bound and yes sabotaged. Those who gave of themselves and was taken advantage of. Women who loved without restraint, trusted blindly, and found themselves on the losing end.

I am the voice of those that have struggled silently and cried out to God in desperation and God through His love and kindness brought freedom, liberty, and release. And although many have hid their testimonies fearful of what others might say about them or how they might be pulled off the pedestal that they have so long occupied, I speak on their behalf.

Yes, brokenness can be mended separation can be painful but you can live again.

Yes, you might be wearing the battle scars of your past. But your scars are a testimony that you were in a battle but not killed. You survived. Your scars don't cry defeat but they scream victory. God turned your mess into a miracle and now you too can declare and rejoice that you were once held captive, a prisoner of war but now by God's grace you're free.

Is it me? Am I losing my mind? Does this person know that he's trying to destroy the very core of my existence? The very thing I've fought my entire life to receive.

Does your mind keep repeating, I thought he was to love me, for better or for worse, for richer or for poorer, in sickness and in health. Or, isn't he was supposed to watch over my soul? If so, why is he trying to destroy me? My faith? My love for God? My love for the church? Or maybe for others it is, I moved here to this place, looking for better. I denied family, friends, other positions to take this one and after I've given them my all, after I've brought this place to a place of excellence, I'm now being told they have no more need for my services. I've trained others and the ones I've trained are now being pushed into my position?

Have you ever been there? In a place where you loved blindly? A place in which you served faithfully and devotedly and instead of being rewarded you were dealt the bitter hand of disloyalty, betrayal and unfaithfulness?

Have you ever been in a place where you thought, no, not thought but you knew without a doubt you were entitled to love, devotion, loyalty, and respect, because you had given your all, you'd poured out your whole body, soul, and mind?

You saw the need, so you chose to drop everything that you had, everything that you believed because you felt the call of God. You felt the pull of love, you felt better opportunities but now the one that you came to help, the one you denied all for, the one you came to encourage, to love and build up was now trying to sabotage you.

Sabotage is such a big word - such a word of betrayal and damage.

Sabotage is defined as the deliberate destruction of property or obstruction of normal operations, as by civilians or enemy, agents in time of war.

The deliberate attempt to damage, destroy, or hinder a cause or activity.

"The Spirit of Sabotage operates as a strong demonic influence that drives people to abort the progress and success of divinely ordained projects, purposes relationships, organization, self, potential, and destinies."

	TO SABOTAGE IS TO:
S	STRATEGICALLY
A	ABORT
B	BEST
O	ONLY
T	TO
A	ACCEPT
G	GREATER
E	ENEMY

Being in ministry, I've seen it so many times, Men and Women of God that will allow the Spirit of Sabotage to completely destroy what God has ordained for them. The Ministry that God has for years used them to establish, then somehow they become their worst enemy, for they will or they will drive others to abort their God ordained destiny.

Being Aware but Dismissing the Warning Signs

One Sunday on my way to Sunday School, just about 2 blocks from my house, I saw a guy walking. He was sweating, with no shirt on and profusely wet. Before I could even wonder what had happened about 60 feet behind him lying in the middle of the road was a beautiful young woman. No doubt at one time the envy of probably so many others but here she was barely clothed, and screaming at the top of her voice. So I pulled up beside her and said, "Honey what's going on? Why are you laying in the middle of this road?" She pointed at the man who had just turned around and said, "He keeps beating me!" I immediately told her to get up and get inside my truck. She slid in and took her place beside my grandsons who were in disbelief.

How could such a beautiful young woman allow herself to be treated like dirt by this, this thing that was supposed to be a representation of a man? She had tattoos all over, her hair was disheveled but she was still beautiful.
I asked, "Where is your family?" She mumbled. I said,

"Baby please don't allow him to beat you again. Please let me drop you off to a family member or friend." She replied, "Right here at this house drop me off." I did, thanking God she had found a place of refuge, I then pleaded with her please don't go back, don't allow him to beat you again and again she mumbled something under her breath and got out.

My granddaughter who was sitting in the front with me said, "Grandma, she's going back, she's going back to where he is." I kept driving not looking back and I told them that's what they do, the enslaved will return to their captor, their master, their enemy.

She had been made aware that this is not normal but she dismissed her warning sign.
That could've been her last opportunity before he killed her or she killed him. She was dependent upon, loyal to, and in love with her enemy - the one that's sabotaging her.

Still devoted to a person that's not devoted to you. Trying to make something work, when it's one sided. Being loyal to disloyalty. Sleeping with the enemy, ignoring the warning signs that no doubt were not visible when she began her fall. Falling into the trap of the Enemy, unaware. Becoming a prey to the enemy.

The best definition I found for prey is - a living thing that is eaten by another living thing. That's what happens with the spirit of Sabotage. You become consumed by your Saboteur. The Saboteur (the one who engages in sabotage) will conceal their true identity because of the consequences of their actions.

They will not reveal who they are or what they're up to. So you will find yourself falling into the trap of the enemy unaware. Thinking this is the best thing in the world.

Blindly, you'll find yourself going against your better judgment. Feeling like - He didn't really mean to do this to me. If I just do this, he'll love me more. I don't like what he's making me do but he loves me, so I'll just do this to get his approval. It's painful but I'll do it because I can trust him. I hate it - It's detesting - it's destroying me on the inside - but I depend on him to have my back.

Is it uncomfortable? Is it bringing you under condemnation? Do you feel yourself scrubbing yourself over and over again because you don't feel clean? Do you feel yourself repenting and saying I'm sorry over and over again - while knowing you're going to return to your Saboteur? Do you feel you're being eaten alive, consumed against your will but you write it off as things will get better?

Becoming a POW

Are you now in the place where you've recognized that this is not the norm? You want to break free and you've tried but there's no release. Have you succumbed to your Saboteur? Feeling as if you've fought long enough and can't fight any longer. What's the use? I'm going to be defeated? No more strength to fight. You've become imprisoned, a prisoner, bound and can't break free in your own will.

When your cry becomes greater than your will, sometimes when you don't have strength within yourself to walk away or the strength anymore to fight; God will force your captor to release you. Your constant cry to be released will come up before God and although you can't break free, He will command your enemy to release you. Sometimes when we experience a divorce, job loss, breakup of a relationship that we've invested years and time into - we see it as a great loss. But could it in fact be that it was holding you captive, keeping you from walking in destiny, keeping you from being all that you created to be - and God was now forcing your captor to release you

A dear friend told me, during one of the worst times of her life. A time when she didn't know that God had a plan for her life. A time of pain and bondage. When she was involved with a married man that would not let her go. A time when she found herself crying out for release because she could not find within herself the strength to break free. That her captor whispered to her - God told me to let you go - the call He has on your life cannot be tampered with or hindered. God said if I don't release you, He's gonna destroy me.

Wow, how can a man that knows not the Lord, proclaim such a statement? God speaks to all of His creatures. Those that know him and those that don't.

To declare Release - Means God is fighting in your behalf. When you have no more strength - When you can't do it - at the time when you felt hopeless - God began to fight for you. He defended you your cry for deliverance, your cry for help became louder than your will.

Luke 13:12 - And when Jesus saw her, he called her to him, and said unto her, Woman, thou art loosed from thine infirmity.

> "This woman had no more strength to fight. Jesus saw her and knew she had been in this condition for 18 years. He heard her precious cries and saw her tears. Even when she didn't open her mouth. Her cries of desperation and release from her bondage was louder and stronger than her will, for her will had been broken. She had been bent and broken so long that she had accepted this condition as the norm. But Jesus saw her. He did not just see her, (to look upon) but He saw her (the depth of her pain, her brokenness, that was hidden from others) and said, "Woman thou art loosed.""

You're freed from your captor, the Saboteur. The one that's keeping you from walking in the fullness of your destiny. You can't be all that God wants you to be bound up and enslaved.

Why is My Release So Painful?

Release can be painful because you've made your pain, your promise. You felt this was what you were entitled to. Nothing more, nothing less. You don't deserve any more than this. You don't deserve, Great, Better or Best. You're losing the man that has cheated on you and brought you nothing but heartache, embarrassment and pain - so why is it so painful? Why am I still longing and craving for him? It's because you have become bound and attached to him, physically, emotionally and spiritually. All area's that you were attached, must now be broken and you must be released from them.

Separation is Painful

A person can have a nasty, ugly cancer growing on them. It's disgusting and killing you and you want it removed but guess what? When it's removed, although it was the vilest thing in the world - the separation is still painful because it had been attached to you. It will heal. As the days go by, the pain will become less and less severe and then one day you will wake up and there's no pain.

Then you could have been fired from that job, that neglected you and tried to keep you oppressed and depressed - they hired others after you and promoted them over you - and now you're free from them - but why is it so painful?

What about you've finally felt the release from that church that you weren't free in. You had no liberty. Your spirit did not connect and you had been forcing yourself and trying to make things happen. Because you weren't happy, they made you more uncomfortable. You were most miserable and they took every opportunity to sabotage you.

So why is it, that now that you're gone, you still want to hear what's going on there? Why does it concern you anymore?

Recognize and Release It

The Spirit of Sabotage comes to bind you and destroy your freedom. The Spirit of Sabotage keeps you from being who you were destined and created to be. It's a distraction, a detour in your road. It keeps you held up and consumed so much so with you and your issues that you're of no use to those that are really depending upon you.

The Spirit of Sabotage makes you feel as if you're running in place, not getting anything accomplished. You feel as if you're being destroyed - eaten alive. You keep giving and others keep taking. They take credit for your work, your ideas, your vision, and leave you thinking but what about me? They keep you close enough to suck and draw the very life from you but far enough not to have to give of themselves.

The Spirit of Sabotage makes you isolate yourself from your family, friends and those that you know have your best interest at heart.
They constantly try to persuade you that they're all that you have and need. Slowly but surely you see them eating away at your Character - that that you once stood far you're not as confident as you once were. Everything now, has to go through them.

But Release and Breakthrough begins with:
    Acknowledging - this is not me,
    Asking yourself - Who or what have I become?

Release and Breaking free begins with:

Trusting and listening to yourself- Listen to that inner witness on the inside. The Holy Spirit and our conscience always warns us. Before we begin to descend we must first discern we must purpose beforehand that we will take heed to the warning of the Holy Spirit and others.

If what you're being encouraged, swayed, or wooed to do is uncomfortable and brings conviction and condemnation, put it off quickly and completely - don't pretend it will eventually become easier - it will not grow on you. Ask those around you, those that you can confide in - true believers, true friends. Those that will not tell you what you want to hear but those that will tell you the truth. If necessary make an appointment with a godly leader or person of truth that you don't know personally. Therefore they want sugar coat the truth and want mind offending you.

Become accountable- My husband, when he first accepted Christ as his Lord and Savior, was so determined to walk a consistent godly lifestyle that he asked brothers new in the faith and those that were consistent in their walk also, to hold him accountable. If they did not see him, call him. If he seemed to be getting slack, encourage and motivate him. If he seemed to be sliding back, bring him to the carpet and remind him of his commitment.

Then make daily confessions- Decree what the will of God is for you. Talk to yourself (yes, its okay) Remember the woman with the issue of blood, said to herself - If I can just touch the hem of Jesus garments I shall be made whole. Then - Ask yourself am I right now at this present time the better or worse? Be truthful, would you admire who you are right now, if it was in your closest friend or loved one?
Well why tolerate it.

Then Outline steps to break free- The Prodigal son, while in the hog pen **came to himself (Come to**

yourself) - then he came up with a step by step plan to break out of his sin cycle, his rock bottom dilemma, he said:

Step #1:	I'm getting up from this place.
Step #2:	I'm going back to my father's house.
Step #3:	I'm going to repent and tell my father I know I've sinned against heaven and you and I'm no more worthy to be called your son.
Step #4:	I'm going to humble myself and ask him to just make me a hired servant.

And the bible says, "And he arose, and came to his Father, but when he was yet a great way off, his Father saw him, and had compassion and ran and fell on his neck and kissed him. And the Father said to his servants, Bring forth the best robe, and put it on him; and put a ring on his hand, and shoes on his feet and bring the fatted calf and kill it and let us eat and be merry, For this my son was dead, and is alive again; he was lost and is found."

Freedom gives life. Freedom will allow you to walk in your God ordained destiny.

When the Spirit of Sabotage is broken and you're released:
> You can live again.
> You can breathe again.
> You can love again.

You can Worship again.

But now it is with no weights, no strings, and no bondages.

There is Freedom and Liberty when Christ sets you free.

John 8:36 - So if the Son sets you free, you will be free indeed.

Escape to Freedom
By: Shadawn Parker

Shadawn Parker

nthemidst89@gmail.com
http://ariseministries7.wix.com/blog

This story is for you, for all the brokenhearted people who have suffered at the hands of someone in their lives, someone who you have trusted but have betrayed that trust. This is a story for all the little girls and young women who felt like they were enslaved to their misery with no end at sight. This is a story for those who feel like they are stuck in their situation and who are struggling to free themselves from this place even when the exit door is right before them. This is a story for all who have been abused in every way imaginable by the ones that we love and adore. This is a story for all of you who have been a prisoner in your own mind and is screaming inside for someone to set you free. This is for you who have struggled to stay free in your mind even when you have escaped your situation physically. This is a story for you who felt like the only way you can escape is through ending your life. This is a story for you who have survived from the Hell you were placed in who are in need of a healing savior, the ultimate healer and deliverer, Jesus Christ. I write this to encourage you that your suffering will not last always. That God can be your light when it seems like you are surrounded by darkness. There is light at the end of this tunnel, so I encourage you to stay strong and never stop fighting for yourself physically and mentally. God gives us hope that one day we will be free, whether it be in this world or the next.

Lying on my bed with my eyes closed, I see a scene of a little girl laughing her heart out, jumping for joy, and talking a mile per hour while playing with friends and family. This scene reminds me of the days where I was absolutely free, free from burden, free from pain, and free to be just me. I cherish these memories of that little girl, these snapshots of freedom, and they make me smile. Even if they were short-lived.

I had many happy family times at my great-grandmother's house, but once my dad stopped working long hours and had more free time, things began to change for me. In my father's presence, I no longer felt free. With every direct order from him, I felt like I was in the military, always stiff with fear of being physically disciplined for doing something wrong. I followed his directions to the point that if he let me taste his soda and told me to stop drinking, I would stop immediately and spill the soda all over my shirt. This feeling of being oppressed by my dad followed me from childhood into early adulthood.

I also battled being ostracized and bullied from elementary school until middle school, so I was not only oppressed at home but in school by my peers as well. I felt like I had nowhere to run and no place to be myself and find peace, especially as I spent much less time with my extended family than I used to. I felt alone and oftentimes depressed. I wasn't a lively, outgoing free spirit anymore. I was a quiet, introverted little girl who lost her voice.

The feeling of being trapped increased when my father began physically abusing me when I was around 12 years old. My earliest memory of that involved a summer school program offering a lot of educational and artistic activities, including ballroom dancing. I had never done that before and having a deep love for dance, I was excited to try it. As we learned the dance, I also learned we would later perform it for family and friends and needed parental permission. I knew immediately that my dad would never give me permission, because I would be dancing with a boy, so I had no choice but to drop out of the class. It didn't matter how much I wanted to participate because I knew my father: even though ballroom dancing was innocent, I would get in serious trouble for doing it.

But at the end of the summer program, the students begged me to fill in for a female dancer who missed the dress rehearsal. I figured it was only one day and could not hurt anything, so I did it. Of course, my father picked that one day to show up at the program early and saw me dancing with the boy. He was livid, and on the way home, he mumbled that he was going to beat my a-s-s. Even though I was scared of what was coming, I believed I deserved it because I screwed up.

When we got home, my dad brought me in front of my mother and made me show her how I danced with the boy. I felt humiliated, exposed, and mocked by something that mattered to me. At the end of it all, my dad made me take off all of my clothes then he beat me with a belt. I was so brainwashed and controlled by my dad that I accepted my punishment and did not question his actions.

As I got older, he would hit me if I said something that he did not like. He called it "being smart," which really meant I was sharing a different opinion of whatever we were talking about. Even as a young adult, I feared he might hit me in the face at any moment if I expressed any thought that was not in line with his beliefs. That fear made me not want to speak, so I said as little as possible. Being trapped and unheard made me feel like I had completely lost who I really was.

I lost even more of myself when my father began sexually abusing me, creating a whole different level of oppression. The first incident actually occurred after I finally told him I was being bullied in school among other things. Instead of supporting me, he became upset because I kept that part of my life a secret. He didn't trust my word anymore because I was a liar, so he needed to "check" to see if I was actually a virgin as I claimed. I was scared of what it meant to "check me" but knew I could not stop him, so I submitted to his decision. Even though I was screaming inside, it was like a heavy hand covered my voice while he penetrated me with his finger. In my mind, I wasn't a virgin anymore, but it would take years before I realized what he did was rape.

This incident was the start of constant surveillance from my dad. In high school, I was forced to take an audio recorder with me every day for a year. Because of that, I wouldn't talk about anything deep or let anyone talk to me about anything important because my words weren't safe and I wanted to respect my friends' privacy. My dad always interrogated me, asking for my secrets and the ones others shared with me. I felt like I had no control, like I had to tell him everything or there would be serious consequences.

When I was in college, my dad installed cameras throughout the house, GPS on my phone, and spyware on my computer without my knowledge. The worst part? He told me because of his unique relationship with God, God was telling him everything I was doing when he wasn't around. And because I knew my dad had a strong relationship with God, I believed him. Not only was I being oppressed by my father, but God was helping him do it! That belief poisoned my relationship with God for a time because I believed He was helping my dad.

The sexual abuse continued through these years, and I grew more and more trapped and confused. By this point, my dad started giving me massages where he would eventually touch my crouch or fondle my breast. I felt every touch beyond my skin, heard his every breath in my whole body, and cried out in my head, "When will this end?" I felt trapped in my own body with no defenses left. When the touching became unbearable, I would either get up or tell my dad that I was finished with the massage, but only after the damage was done.

What kept me somewhat sane during my father's abuse was actually my faith in God. After learning my dad's "unique relationship with God" was actually technology, I wanted to try to trust God again. My faith slowly became stronger, and I started believing God could help me. After hearing a particular sermon, I remember writing in my journal that I was still stuck in my Egypt, a slave in my own home, and that God would deliver me from this terrible place. I prayed diligently for the abuse to end or to experience some relief. One time I prayed that my father would stop forcing me to kiss him because it was becoming unbearable. The next day my father told me that we were not going to kiss anymore. Even though there were different incidents afterwards, I knew God heard my prayer and that gave me hope.

But that hope wasn't strong enough to stop me from being depressed. Squeezing my teddy bear for comfort, I lay awake crying at night for all the pain I was in and the heavy, secret burden I was carrying. I felt it was taking God too long to deliver me and started wondering if either suicide or killing my dad was the only way I could escape the torment. What was the point of living if I couldn't be free?

My friend Mariana* was the only friend who knew about my father's abuse, and when I confessed my desire to hurt myself, she put her foot down; either I would tell my mom what was going on or she would. Weeks before I told my mother, I felt like God wanted me to know He had a plan for my life and directed me to Jeremiah 29:11. So no matter what happened, I would be okay.

To warm up to telling my mother, I tried to tell Kennedy*, my long-time mentor who didn't know about the abuse. But I was so nervous that the words wouldn't come out. Thankfully she guessed the truth before I actually said it, and to this day, I believe this was a sign from God that He was with me. Kennedy agreed to support me in telling my mother, so one day in a private room at church with Kennedy standing outside the room, I told my mom about the abuse. I was terrified of what might happen, but my mother seemed to believe me, like she was going to protect me. Her response lifted a huge weight from my shoulders and I believed my mom's involvement would free me from further abuse.

But that did not happen.

My mother did confront my father that day when I wasn't around. But whatever happened during that conversation did not result in my father changing or my mother vowing to protect me. Instead my mother brought me into their sitting room where my father prayed that I would learn forgiveness and how to let things go. Once again, my father got his way, and now he manipulated my mother into not fully believing me.

I had never felt so rejected and depressed in my entire life. That terrible burden of pain and oppression returned to my shoulders even heavier than before. I was backed up in a small corner where there was no real escape and truly feared my dad would just keep abusing me with no end in sight. But even in that darkest time of my life, God reminded me of his promise again in Jeremiah 29:11, while watching the movie, *Soul Surfer*, with my sisters. He had a plan for my life, to give me hope and a future. I held on to that verse with every hope in my heart, believing that one day I would be free.

Two weeks after I told my mom about the abuse, I realized there was another way for the abuse to end: I could leave. I could leave my home and all it's suffering behind. With this idea in mind, I asked God over and over again what I should do and heard him say multiple times that it was time for me to leave. I shared the idea with Kennedy, and she gladly helped me make secret arrangements to leave.

Even though I felt like I needed to leave for my own protection, I was terrified. I had no idea how to survive in the outside world. I was only sure of a place to stay for a couple of days, so I feared not having a permanent and safe home. But in my heart, God kept asking me to take His hand and walk on the water with Him and let Him guide me into the unknown. I might have been blind to what would come but God knew everything and promised to take care of me and lead me in the right direction.

The weekend of April 14, 2012, my entire family was away, and I saw my chance. I packed two suitcases of clothes and books I needed for school. Kennedy sent one of her friends to pick me up and take me to Evelyn's house. When she wrapped me in her welcoming embrace, I knew my dad would never get the chance to hurt me again. I knew my pain would not just end with me leaving home and that I had a very long journey to healing ahead of me. But I also knew God had heard my prayer and delivered me from my Egypt. I knew I was free. But physical freedom, I would soon learn, did not equal emotional and psychological freedom. Don't get me wrong: there were major, positive differences between my old home and this temporary new one. Evelyn and her family created a safe, stable environment for me. They treated me like one of their own, never judged me, and I truly felt I had been adopted by a new family.

Despite being surrounded by so much love and peace, I still felt depressed and lonely because I didn't think anyone there could truly relate to me and all my pain. Nightly flashbacks and other PTSD symptoms attacked me so often that I felt as if I were still being abused. Though physically free, I was trapped in a mental prison, afraid of men in general and terrified my father would find me and forcibly take me back home. Yet I wanted to protect him from exposure to outside authorities or other family members, so none of my extended family would learn where I was or why I'd left for three more years.

Eventually with Evelyn's help and support, I enrolled in Cairn University in Langhorne, Pennsylvania in the fall of 2012. I maintained contact with my old friends but enjoyed my freedom in a new state. I met new people who showered me in the love of Christ and accepted me for who I presented myself to be. But the "me" I kept hidden would not stay buried for long.

As I began my Christian Counseling lab work, rage, shame, and other powerful emotions bubbled to the surface. I finally realized the sheer horror of my former life at home, and the weight of those feelings shocked and scared me. I got myself into counseling, which was a helpful step toward healing, but I made other choices that weren't so healthy. Like the Israelites in the wilderness, I spent a long time blaming, resenting, and rejecting God. I spat in his face and slapped away His hand away every time He reached out to me. If He was so powerful, then why didn't He stop my abuse before it started? Why did He let it go on so long? And why should I trust Him now?

By my second semester at Cairn, I was succeeding academically yet still struggling personally. Burdened with feelings and flashbacks, I started cutting myself regularly. That habit got so bad that I spent a week in a mental hospital, trying to put a Band-Aid on a wound needing spiritual surgery from the God I had turned my back on. Yet I remembered hearing the children's song "Jesus Loves Me" the entire time I was in the hospital. I didn't think I could hear from God anymore, yet He placed that song in my spirit to say, "I still love you, no matter what."

Though I didn't cut myself again for almost two years, a longstanding porn and masturbation addiction worsened, prompting me to frequent websites where I could connect with other women via video-chat. I was heading down a sinful slippery slope, yet that song from the hospital never left my heart. Though I deliberately sinned against Him, God showed me so much love and grace I could hardly understand it. He used different friends to stage interventions at critical points in my recovery, their support reminding me that I was not alone anymore. He led me to new doctors who used intense but effective therapies that decreased my PTSD symptoms.

Despite this positive progress, I noticed myself doing impulsive, out-of-character things and having sudden, intense bouts of depression for no apparent reason. I started cutting myself again at the start of my third year at Cairn and eventually attempted suicide. During the recovery process, I found a new psychiatrist who discovered a year-old, undisclosed diagnosis of bipolar disorder. This revelation crystallized so much of my struggle and gave me a handle on my true needs. With a new, stabilizing medication and better understanding, I felt my recovery could truly begin.

After about a month with my new counselor and new medication, God led me to attend a two-week spiritual program called the School of Empowerment. At this gathering of faith-filled people, I received prayer for my issues and felt the heavy chains of mental and emotional bondage break off me. God, my true, eternal Father, gave me a glimpse of His plan for my life and assured me again He would never stop loving me. At some point, I actually felt Him embrace my hand as a father might do when comforting a crying child. God removed so much of the poison from my heart that I was able to dance every day in worship during those two weeks, fully embracing God's love just as it embraced me.

As I sit here, I truly feel free. I feel like I have finally escaped the painful wilderness and entered the Promised Land where God always intended for me to be. Although I know healing is an on-going process, I am confident that whenever I feel broken again, God will always pick me up and mend the broken pieces of my heart.

As part of His plan for my life, God has inspired me to use my experience to heal the brokenhearted in this country and beyond and to help survivors of abuse and trafficking. I am writing and establishing programs for women and teens to express their feelings, particularly with the arts, in a safe, welcoming community. I want to direct them to mentors, counselors, and the ultimate healer, Jesus Christ. Being healed while healing others is a long, winding journey, but as I bask in the peace of my Promised Land, I can say for sure that with God, anything is possible. Especially an escape to freedom.

The Great Deception

By: Xaviera L. Bell

A single touch of the hand intrigued me. It wasn't the touch but the spark that was ignited within me. The conversations that made love to my mind made me fall, it was a whirlwind and my life was shaken up by the twister that you were and I was displaced like a victim that was left abandoned with nothing to run to. You closed a chapter in my life without my permission and you have not allowed me to write my ending because you've kept the book open because you were not equipped to totally walk away. You told me with your actions that spewed like venom on the pages that we created that I wasn't enough for you. The words that were formed by the love that we made were so temporary in this life's chapter that they vanished without a trace and I stand broken with pen in hand trying to remember what we had but it's been enveloped by the harshness of you.

How could 1+1=2 and still be wrong? How could me plus you equal us and still be wrong? How could the beat of my heart pause in my chest and the inhale of oxygen expand my breast at the very thought of you and still be wrong.

I believed you when you held me and the promises that were whispered in my ear that we would build a life and I would be your wife. I, waited for you to arrive at your fullest potential, I was thinking commercial and you were residential. You put us in a box and deprived us of growth because you knew that there was no future to us. You knew that you had no intention to build with me because you weren't skilled enough to see who I really was. I was more than just a body that kept you warm night after night. I was the tear that you released and the prayer that was laid at God's feet on behalf of us. I was your juice but you were too noosed by the concept that love would someday end, so you put me in the category of enemy instead of a lover and a friend.

How could 1+1=2 and still be wrong? How could me plus you equal us and still be wrong? How could the beat of my heart pause in my chest and the inhale of oxygen expand my breast at the very thought of you and still be wrong.

I sit in my thoughts and my feelings and question the validity of you. How could you deceive the very person that saved you from you? How could you decide that it was done without even consulting me? I was supposed to be the answers to your dreams and I never considered that you were a camouflaged nightmare. You know that thing that appeared to be greatness but was just a learned behavior because you had watched enough Lifetime to appear that you had substance, all the while I had settled for a nothing. The emptiness of your apology left me numb and then I realized that this is who you are, empty. I never considered that your emptiness sought me out because I was full of the light that you so desired. And even in your departure you fear returning to an existence without me. Your, I miss you's and I made a mistake text means nothing because you are married to your situation and there's no getting better for you. You can't be better because you are not true to you. You have returned to the hole that you once dug and the hand that I extended is now retracted because I will not save you. I realize that the hole that you created is big enough for two and I refuse to keep you company in the hole you dug for you. The truth is I'm better than you.

But how could 1+1=2 and still be wrong? How could me plus you equal us and still be wrong? How could the beat of my heart pause in my chest and the inhale of oxygen expand my breast at the very thought of you and still be wrong. It's wrong because of the deceit of it all. You created a façade that you were not able to keep up. Being true was too much work for you.

Accountability and compromise was far down your list and while I was enhancing you, you were digging a ditch for me. Secretly. Because a life with you for me was doable and all this time you were planning my emotional funeral. I shudder at the thought that I was almost lost in a situation that was destined for failure and I sit here and I can't pull myself together. Because I'm mad at you and what's ridiculous is that I have to explain why because you have no clue. That's more than enough reason to bounce and be done with you! Forever.

However, through it all I must give thanks that he made me strong enough to recover and save the love that he created in me for another. That the damage that you caused was all for my good and even thought I shouldn't I know that I could, forgive you. Because you're way more damaged than what you thought you did to me. You're flawed beyond repair and the next victim thinks they are getting a bargain but there's no value to you. Like putting money in a pocket and expect a return. There's no getting better and no matter how long they stay on their knees there's no better for you. Even if they weather the storm there is nothing that they could do because you're in control of you, and being common and deceitful is what's desirable for you. I thank God for my experience and this new direction but most of all I thank him for uncovering.. The greatest deception.

Unbreakable

By. Tanisha Grey

Tanisha Grey
tanishan.grey@gmail.com

My name is Tanisha. My story is one of hurt, pain, and mental anguish. Although, I now see it could have been so much worse, but yet, this was still my pain, my story. I am the only girl of five children. I was labeled "spoiled", but I called it privileged. I was privileged to have parents who always took my best interest at heart and struggled day in and day out to protect me as well as provide the best life they could for myself and my brothers. With all that being said; everyone makes mistakes, the mistake that my family made was not taking my feelings into consideration.

Although I was well put together on the outside I was a mess inwardly. I know how it feels when you look in the mirror and not like what you see. You may have felt like these insecurities were limited to you but they're not. I have walked down the same path, allowing the troubles of the past to continue to bring me down. It is my hope that as you turn these pages you know that you're beautiful with all your flaws. I want you to embrace the parts of you that might not seem so beautiful at this moment. Don't allow the painful words of others destroy the way you feel about yourself. The best love is self-love! No matter how torn you may feel you can always be mended. There is no greater strength than overcoming your trails and becoming a better you!

There are many homes that are broken, whether an absent parent or being raised by close relatives. I was fortunate to have both of my parents in the home but often times than not, I felt alone. I am the only girl of five children and the youngest, so that has both its advantages and disadvantages. I was also big for my age and in family that seemed to always be an issue. I often yearned for acceptance and viewed my body in a very negative light. My brothers would make jokes about my weight and my parents just added fuel to the fire. I'm not sure that they knew how much their words really hurt me. When I would look in the mirror and I saw my reflection I didn't like what I saw; from the dark circles around my eyes to how plump my lips were.

Confidence was not instilled in me at an early age. It wasn't until I was older that my mother told me the importance of accepting me. My mother would tell me how much she prayed for a girl but in the same breath tear me down about how fat I was, this gave me a complex and so many insecurities. It's funny how the ones we love can cause us the most pain. My older brother and I have the same father; my three eldest brothers are from my mother's previous marriage. He and I have a good relationship but on the flip side, if anyone could make me feel two feet tall it would be him. I cried so many nights tasting my tears wishing I was someone else. Siblings always quarrel but my parents weren't adamant on correcting him on calling me names and added to my low self-esteem; it's unfortunate because how can one change their behavior if they don't know how deeply it impacts you?

My mother would always compare me to my brothers and I hated it. I felt like I was always in competition with them especially the one that he and I share the same father. My mother and I were always at odds, her favorite phrase to say to me was "two bulls can't rule in the same pen." I understood the statement but on the other hand, I felt like even if she was the authority did that mean I had no voice and the hurtful things she said to me were dismissed because she was my mother? I didn't like being the center of attraction when it came to how I ate and what I looked like.

My father was present but he wasn't as active in my adolescence as I wished he was. There are a lot of single parent homes, but there are also two parent homes where the parent isn't active in their child(ren)'s lives, this was the case in our family. My father was an authoritative figure, he provided financially but when it came to emotions he was a blank slate. He had a great impact on the way I felt about myself. He would talk about how fat I was as well, but he never gave me the assurance that even though I was a little bigger than I should be, I was still beautiful and he loved me. A father's presence is imperative in the growth and development of children, being a provider is necessary but showing love is KEY!

There was always an elephant in the room and that ELEPHANT was me! This was not only figuratively but literally as well, at least that is what I was programmed to believe. I was often the "butt "of the family's jokes and the worse kind, "FAT JOKES". I hated it. My family didn't take into consideration my feelings. Unbeknownst to them; I cried many nights and felt ridiculously awkward within myself. This was more than a phase, I would call it my journey, because it stretched as far as the Nile in my eyes. But I found an escape and that would was poetry. With every encounter, harsh feeling, and disappointment, I made the words flow like water on the pages of my composition book. This was not only therapeutic but also a confidence builder.

Although there were great days, a majority of my days were tough. I can remember my mother saying to me, "You are was sooo fat!" Yes, emphasis on the "O's". It got so bad that I remember watching an episode of "Models Inc." and one of the models were on a casting call but she didn't make the cut because the designer said she was too "fat". She then went in the bathroom after being rejected, turned on the faucet and stood over the toilet, and began sticking her finger down her throat. I thought about this scene long after it was done and concocted in my mind that I could eat the way I wanted and then I would lose the weight. But I wouldn't get off that easy because I hated vomiting. I did my research and found out what I mimicked was the behavior of a bulimic and the lasting effects would be much greater than shedding a few pounds.

Beauty is in the eye of the beholder
But why didn't I see the beauty that was in me
It wasn't that it didn't exist
But these insecurities held me hostage
I was held captive
It was like a smoking gun
Ready to kill
Kill my confidence
Infiltrate on my self-esteem
Demolish my self-worth
Leave me in stage of disappointment
Not owning this body
The landslides
These roadblocks
Built thick like Fort Knox
But I wanted to be a frail jail cell
That held no weight
Locked into my own mind
My own thoughts
Keeping me down
Telling me that I wasn't this beautiful being
Creatively crafted in divine majesty!

I remember my father's favorite line to say to me in his strong Jamaican accent was, " Yuh nahm like a Fahmah ASS" and in layman's terms meant, "You eat like a farmer's ass" boy I hated that. But the most toe clenching irritating moments would be when we would go out to eat and it was my time to order. I would scroll down and dissect the menu, first checking the prices in comparison to what everyone else ordered then how elaborate it was in comparison the rest of the meals, once that was done I was ready to order. But not before I got the rolled eyes from my mother and the PSA telling me not to go overboard in so many words. Now of course I knew my boundaries but this was supposed to be an event. We didn't frequent restaurants (my mother was a good home cooking kind of mother) so when this happened it was definitely an enjoyable experience, but after the looks and I mean what felt like flesh burning stares and the prerequisites for my dinning it just took all the fun out of it.

With all these imperfections at least in my eyes, like many pre-teens I became insecure. I remember looking at magazines in awe of these black women mostly the ones that were of a lighter complexion. I was very fair skin as a child but as I grew older my skin became darker; I suffered from eczema, so I had a lot of light and dark patches. My brother called me "blotchy" and that was my nick name from that point on, but only my best friend and her cousins knew the "inside joke". At that time I didn't see the humor in it because my skin was always a big issue for me coupled with my other insecurities. I viewed lighter complexioned girls and women as beautiful, while my brown skin, scared and hyper-pigmented, was not so lovely. I remember putting powder on my face and the irony of this was that my mother told me when I was around six years old I would tell her that I was white and through school I was coined "the white girl" but that was just because I spoke very proper even among my peers, but looking back it seems as if all these pieces would lead to make my "Insecure Puzzle" and I would continue to try to find the pieces that would make me feel complete.

I really don't remember feeling like I was "beautiful". I was tall for my age and with that came a maturity that shined through not only on the outside but also the way I spoke and carried myself. I would often get the cat calls from older men and be called "sexy". I hated that word. I didn't connect beauty with sexiness, after all, I was young, so being sexy wasn't a compliment to me. I had very large breasts for a young girl and it made me feel ashamed, like I was only viewed "sexy" due to my bosom and my facial features didn't matter, I wanted to be considered BEAUTIFUL, PRETTY! While some would love to be blessed with such a nice "rack" I hid in shame because the attention was too much for me at that time; this further increased my insecurities. I also had what I thought was the biggest balloon lips ever (what was I thinking, people actually pay for the lips I hated so much back then, but NOW, I love me some them). There wasn't much talk about self-love in our household. I was often told by my mother that she loved me but not really the importance of accepting myself for who I was and what I looked like.

My family was very judgmental of me. My mother and I were always at odds. It felt like WW3 at least four times a week in our house. I will admit I could be very rude at times, stubborn, and didn't take direction well, but my mother seemed to always be angry, miserable even. In hindsight, I now know that she went through her own pain and struggles and having five children wasn't easy, although her first three were grown she still had a pre-teen and teenager to deal with. Besides my poor self-image, I often felt unloved by my mother, regardless of what she did for me and that was truly her ALL! She always compared me to my brothers and told me hurtful things like she wished I never was born, but on any given Sunday she would tell me how much she prayed for a girl, this was disturbing to a 12 year old. I often felt like my life was meaningless, if my mother loved me then why would she wish I wasn't born? If I were her prized possession why in that moment, that second, she didn't want me anymore? These words would be imbedded in my mind and I would never forget it.

Living my life with inferiority complexes often complicated things. Looking in the mirror seeing the reflection brought a lack of satisfaction. My mother was very pivotal in the way I viewed myself, I felt resentment towards her because she didn't instill in me at that time in my life "CONFIDENCE". Due to the constant scrutiny I felt inferior, there was always something lacking and I was in a race to obtain it. There was a point where she didn't want to admit that the hurtful things she would say, like calling me out of my name, saying that I was a "Devil out of Hell" molded a monster. That monster in me lead to self-doubt, lead to me hating myself. I was called a whore before the male anatomy even touched mine, much less penetrated. I cried uncontrollably. I remember calling her a "Bitch" and telling her I hated her, I felt so low. My mother and I had many battles but she was still someone I looked up to despite her hurtful words. I always wanted to please her and it just never seemed to be enough. I excelled in school just to hear a job well done and believe within myself it was true. Although my parents always acknowledged my accomplishments, they also cut me down as soon as they picked me up. She would always say "sky is the limit baby girl" but what she didn't know was I didn't want to be a "star pupil" but their "start child".

Sticks and stones might break your bones
But your words don't hurt me
Lies!
Who ever made that saying must have pulled the wool over the eyes
Of anyone who actually believed it
Your words were damaging
They molded self-hate
They created a complex
The lack of self-worth entered
With every ignorant statement
They cut like a double edged sword
With each syllable
Every word that rolled off of your tongue
Sliced me to pieces
Did you know that I hated myself?
Did you know I wished I was never born?

But those were words spoken out of your mouth
You breaded the idea in my mind
It festered like a sore
Then it spread like a cancer
Do you know how much you hurt me?

I have overcome the hurt I felt from my family, because when you are unaware of certain things you are unable to change. I have forgiven my mother for her hurtful words, because through it all she continued to be by my side, although she didn't know the extent of my pain, she was always there. I accepted the faults of my father and forgave him for the things he didn't give me; like the sense of security that surpassed the knowledge that he could and would defend me at all costs, but it was the security knowing I was loved by him unconditionally. He is a great part of my life and I thank him for all his help. He now has three grandchildren that he seems to be living vicariously through, because he wasn't there for my brother and I. I have a best friend in my brother, he is still a little rough around the edges but we have a bond that is unbreakable. I now have found love, although it took years of hurt and many tear drops to get there we did it! He reminds me all the time of my greatness, strength, drive, and dedication, not to mention that I am beautiful and he loves me to the moon and back. I have two sons and one girl that follows and watches my every move as I did to my mother. She reminds me so much of myself it's scary, but what I refuse to do, is allow her to feel less than her strong, beautiful, intelligent self EVER! I have instilled the same confidence in my eldest son; I remind him that his chocolate skin is that of a God and he is perfect just the way he is. I never want my children to feel the way I felt as a child, nor do I want it to follow them through adulthood. I think the best thing you can give a child is your love and attention, finances and stability are necessary but building them up at all cost should never be secondary. I overcame a lot of pain but I know I went through it for a reason. The woman I see now isn't the same awkward little girl or insecure young lady in her twenties, I'm stronger despite the pain that I have gone through.

I can't take any credit for this strength or the gift I possess, because if it wasn't for this God I serve, it would mean NOTHING! We often question and wonder WHY ME? Well why not you? We all have a road to travel and a cross to bear but it is up to us to seek him and ask for the help, the change. We are nothing without God and I thank my mother for being a praying woman. I would wonder why she would be crying while she prayed and I would even become frightened when she started to go into praise but I now know why. I studied her every move, and that was one of her characteristics I embodied. I am a PRAYING WOMAN! It is my belief that God is the orchestrator of all of our lives. He allowed me to experience this pain so I could tell my story and hopefully help someone who felt as if they were alone and no one has travelled down the same road they have.

These "growing pains" brought me to the realization that I was more than my cup, waist, and hip size. It forced me to grow a thicker layer of skin, after all, if I felt hurt by the words of my loved ones, how could I face a world full of vipers who would never give a second thought to the way I felt. In order to cope with all these emotions and thoughts of doubt that I was facing, I began to pour my emotions out with written words, in my journal. I always felt like a load was taken off of my shoulders once I wrote my confessions down in my book. At times I just wanted to scream and tell my parents and brothers I hated the jokes, being singled out, but what would their reaction be? How could I say that at times I felt like crawling in a hole and just staying there, or that I began to hate the person I saw in the mirror because I just didn't feel I was good enough, pretty enough. I found healing in writing down my thoughts, this was my release. The insecurities I found physically became nothing in comparison to my writing; I suddenly became validated. My beauty was now in the words I wrote. There was suddenly a level of confidence, that I didn't know was there, and I loved it. Please remember your body is your temple, take care of it, never be ashamed of who you are and if you don't like what you see, make healthy choices in order to get those results. I now know that everything is for a reason and I'm a better person because of my STRUGGLES!

Standing in the Storms of Life

By: Wryshona Isaac

Wryshona Isaac
luvlivrespectfullyfe@gmail.com

My name is Wryshona Isaac. I was born and raised in Jacksonville, Florida in a Christian home. I am a mother of 3 girls and 1 boy. As a child, I've always enjoyed reading and writing. Notebook paper, pens, and pencils were always near me. I knew deep down inside of me since I was a child that I wanted to write. I entitled my story "Standing in the Storms of Life" because there are times when we have to be still and let God be God.

I'm writing my story as an encouragement to any soul that has ever felt like giving up on life. When I was chosen to tell my story, I struggled with which part of my life to let you in within the confines of a short story. I have faced so many hardships that choosing just one particular storm was not an easy task. I am here to testify that God is real and his love is real.

My pain produced my purpose and my purpose is to share my story. Somethings that I have been through should have destroyed me but by God's grace and his mercy and unfailing *love* is the reason I am still standing. So I encourage any of my readers no matter what storms, trials, or tribulations that come your way, *Never* quit. Pray without ceasing and give it all to *our Lord*.

Love, Wryshona Isaac

I always think on things of the past. The good times are great memories. The bad times are just what they are bad and we may want to block that from our memory. However, we should use the bad moments we have endured to guide our future decisions. There is always a lesson to be learned in every situation. When you learn from the bad times or mistakes it will grow your character and make you stronger. I pray that as I reflect back on some moments in my life, that I touch a soul and give them inspiration to continue on this journey we call LIFE.

In February of 2007, I was shocked to find out that I would be expecting my fourth child. I found out while I was at work. My cousin went and bought a pregnancy test because I couldn't stay woke at work. I just knew I wasn't pregnant because I had just had a baby five months prior. I had many mixed emotions about the pregnancy. I already had three beautiful girls and I was in the middle of planning a wedding with my fiancé and the father of all my children. I thought an abortion would be the answer as selfish as it sounds, I could not afford and wasn't ready to have another child because my last daughter I had the previous year in September.

I made an appointment to the abortion clinic against the wishes of my cousin. I could not sleep that night. I cried a lot and prayed a lot. In my heart I didn't want to kill my baby. My mother-in-law said, "Shona please don't do it, I know that is my grandson." My heart was so heavy but still I chose to go. When I woke up the next morning I remember my kids' dad being so angry with me about the decision. My mom picked me up bright and early. The ride to the clinic was quiet my mind was racing and full of thoughts that would not let up. I cried the whole ride. The memories of that day are still like yesterday. I am blinking back the tears as I am typing my story.

I walked in the clinic and to my surprise it looked like any other doctors office. There were people everywhere including children and everyone appeared to be happy. I felt like I was the only one that was out of place. I expected it to be solemn and a sad looking atmosphere, it was a place where Gods' creations were being taken and ripped out of their mothers' womb. I filled out my paperwork and paid my fee to take a life. All the while I am praying in my head. Lord if you give me a way out I am taking it. If this isn't your will give me an out. I heard my name being called, I got up and slowly walked to the back where several other patients were. I am still praying Lord please help me out of this. I had pressure from some people in my life that didn't think me having my baby would be a good idea. I was crying and trying to hide it but I was in pain behind this decision. I was then taken into another room and was told to undress and put on a hospital type gown. In this particular room was an ultrasound machine and a long table with the white paper on top. I did what was requested of me and sat on the table and waited for the doctors.

Once the doctors came in the room I was told to lay back as they put the cold jelly on my belly to see the life growing inside of me. Then it happened the doctor looked at me and asked, "Do you have a cold?" My answer was, "No." He then stated, "You are too congested for us to perform this procedure today. I need you to be able to breath on your own. We are going to reschedule you because as a doctor I don't feel comfortable putting you to sleep, we need you to be able to breath on your own." My prayers had been answered. I got dressed and high tailed it out of that clinic and I knew that I would not be going back.

I got through the pregnancy and it was a pretty normal pregnancy. Minus the mental anguish that I went through because my kids' father decided to have an affair.

September 26, 2007, the day before my daughter's first birthday, I gave birth to what I thought was a healthy baby boy. After having him I had a surgery to tie my tubes to prevent any future pregnancy. Everything went smoothly. My son spent a lot of time in the nursery. The day we were being discharged I had a feeling that something wasn't right. I asked the nurse if my son had any bowel movements. This might seem unusual but I didn't change one diaper while we were admitted and that didn't sit well with me. The nurse told me that they had some recorded bowel movements in the nursery. I believed her.

On the day that we were discharged we went to my mother-in-law's house to spend the night. Everything seemed normal, however, my son wasn't feeding like I thought he should be. To many this might not have been an issue but this coupled with the fact that he had not had a bowel movement concerned me. My mother-in-law told me to watch him closely because it was not normal, he should have used the bathroom by now. In my mind he wasn't eating a lot so that was my reasoning for him not using the bathroom. The next day I decided to go home to my apartment to get into the routine of things. I got home and got settled in and started to fix my kids dinner. I picked my baby up out of the crib to change him and get him comfortable before I ate. I laid him on the bed and unwrapped him and immediately knew that something was terribly wrong.

His stomach was so big he looked like the children on the commercials when they are asking for people to donate money for food. I picked up the phone and called my mother and started to cry. It was a rainy day and I was a wreck. I said to my mom," Something is wrong with my baby!" I asked her if I should drive him to the hospital or call the paramedics. I called the paramedics and they immediately rushed us off. I was crying and begging them not to let him die. I couldn't have any more children and he was my only son. The anguish and fear that set in during that ambulance ride was enough to make any mother weak. The fact of not knowing if her child would live or die. I know that it is a little ironic being I started off in the abortion clinic. But one thing was certain, my heart never wanted to kill my baby.

This began an ongoing series of surgeries and test. He had an exploratory surgery the following morning after being admitted. They removed his appendix because there was inflammation. The doctors did not find a hole in his stomach or intestines as they originally thought. It took about a month before they finally had a diagnosis. HIRSCHSPRUNG DISEASE!! The first thing I thought to myself is what is this really? Google was my friend. It gave me information on the disease but nothing could ever prepare me for what my family would endure. In a nutshell this disease is one that affects the intestines. We have cells that tells our bodies when we should use the bathroom inside of our intestines. My son's body did not develop the ganglion cells.

This disease affects every day living. To help you understand imagine not being able to make it to the bathroom when you have diarrhea every day at least 4 to 5 times a day. Toilet training was impossible because he had no control over his bowels. We didn't take a lot of trips anywhere because of his situation. My baby wore pull ups from the age of 2 until 6 years of age. Honestly, there were times when I did not have the money to buy pull ups. I would steal them just to get by. I applied to get disability benefits and they have been denied three times already. I don't understand that but I won't stop fighting. He had his third surgery at the age of 6. This was a major surgery and I was nervous. He was having a mickey button put in, the surgery was successful. He currently has this on the side of his navel. It allows for me to flush his bowels. I use a liquid laxative, a mix of pure glycerin and sodium chloride. It gave us some control as far as going out a little more publicly.

I can still remember when my son could go out and play without being embarrassed about using the bathroom on himself and smelling bad. He still has accidents sometimes daily or every other day, it is not as many accidents and that gives him some normalcy. He just recently had it accidentally snatched out while playing a Florida game called Alligator in the pool. My fear manifested when I received that call. They rushed my son by ambulance to the E.R. thankfully he was ok. They put a temporary tube in the hole to keep it open until a new button was ordered. The doctors took about a week and half to replace it. There are still countless doctors' appointments. When my child gets a stomach virus it is actually worse than a child with a normal digestive system and he ends up in the hospital. A virus that last 48 hours usually last for at least a week.

I want to bring awareness to this disease. I had no prior knowledge of the disease until my son was diagnosed. I chose this part of my life to share because I know there are other people going through this storm. Having a child with an illness, or even a disability isn't easy and it takes a special person to handle situations like mine. It probably would have been easier to have had the abortion but that wasn't God's will for my life or my son. My heart was for my son to live. He definitely knew who he was before he was formed in my womb and I am thankful and I am grateful to God for allowing me the chance to be his mother and the mother of my three girls.

I am a single mom with very little income at the moment and not much help from their dad. My girls are my backbones as well they have always been right there for me and my son. I want you to know that God is there every step of the way and He will NEVER leave nor FORSAKE you. Learn to speak life over your situations, learn to speak life to yourself. Remember that words are powerful. Remember that GOD is all knowing and he loves you. As I was in the process of writing my testimony, God stepped in again. I was blessed with a full time job with great benefits. I urge you to look for the good in every situation. God is God and he is sovereign. He will make ways when there seems to be no way for you.

This storm isn't over but I trust and believe God for total healing over my son. I believe that healing will come through my obedience. I have a platform to tell single parents that it may be hard but God is going to work it all out. My son is an active boy and he doesn't let his condition stop him. I taught my son how to pray and exercise big faith in God. He knows that God is a healer and by his stripes my son will be healed totally. My prayer is for whoever is reading this that you saw the hand of God in my life.

Prayers get answered. They may not come like you want them but his answer is THE answer. It is my belief that you could never know who you are without trials testing your faith to build your character, or where you stand when it comes to your faith if you don't experience these storms of life. Sometimes they may feel more like fiery trials or troubled waters, you have to remember to keep God first. Pray without ceasing always (I Thessalonians 5:17). When things feel like they are out of control relax and remain calm. God is able and is in complete control. It is imperative that you stay in prayer for your salvation and protection. My storm isn't over but I learned how and what to do while waiting on God to answer my prayers.

While I wait I am telling my story spreading awareness and encouraging you ladies to stand strong in God and he will always be there with you standing in the middle of your storms and even till the end of time. He wants you to come to him and cast your cares on him the one that cares for you. MAN WILL FAIL YOU, put your trust and hope in the ONE that CREATED you his name is ELOHIM. ALPHA and OMEGA.

It is my prayer that God blesses the person reading my testimony. Father let them know that with you ALL is possible. Whatever storm is raging in their lives let them know that you are the storm calmer. When things are raging all around them Lord give them your peace to stand in that storm. AMEN

Seven Times Hotter

By: Xaviera L. Bell

Xaviera L. Bell

EXODUS PROJECT FOUNDER
BEL EKRI PUBLISHING CO-FOUNDER

AUTHOR OF
WALKING IN THE FULLNESS OF YOU

Exodus_Project@outlook.com
www.belekripublishing.com

When toiling with the thought of starting the Exodus Project I had you in mind. I weighed my options. I thought what would happen to her if she didn't get the opportunity to see first-hand that hurt just isn't that painful always. I can remember sitting in my own despair. I remember the saltiness of my tears mixed with the bitterness of my own self-appointed defeat. How intoxicating and heavy it was just to carry the burden of being hurt from day to day.

I know personally how painful it is to have an event to transpire that changes the total direction of your life. I know how it feels for a chapter of your life to be closed and you didn't give permission for the scene to end. I know what it is like to wait on something that never arrives and how each day you will your heart to stop because it's so extremely damaged that the very fact that it is beating is miraculous. I also know how it feels to wake up and be able to breathe a little less labored.

Throughout this turbulent time of my life I realized an important fact. I realized that this snapshot in time does not determine who I am, what I am worth, or what I will become after it's over.. And it will be over.

I chose to depart my place of despair and I encourage you to do the same. You deserve it. You are worth it!

Never underestimate your ability to recreate yourself. Every weak place provides you with an area of opportunity. Every break or bruise allows you to mend. Every day of rain gives you the expectation of sunshine.

You are phenomenal and my expectation for you is to be better than you were yesterday, to create a new you for tomorrow, and live the life you can live on today.

Great things are ahead for you. If you give up now.. You'll never see all the wonderful things that you are destined to reap. Keep going!

There were so many inconsistencies that I should not have ignored. I should have ran before I was sucked in too deep. I stayed because I thought that the man that I had devoted years to was the man that was going to be my husband. I wondered why not only was I blinded by love but everyone that knew us was fooled into believing that we were going to be a dynamic couple in ministry. There were people that were rooting for us and then there were many who were praying against us.

There is nothing that you can do with a man that has another woman of influence in his ear. When I look back I recognize that I was fighting a losing battle for years. No matter how much I tried to fix him or make his life comfortable, I may have temporarily had his heart but I did not have influence over him. Oh, the dangers of that.

When a man shows you who he is, believe him. When he exposes things during pillow talk, know they are true. One day he said to me, "My spiritual mother said that I can't marry you because you'll ruin my ministry like my mother did my father's." I became immediately offended. My response to him was, "I don't think that it's wise to take advice about marriage from someone that has never had a husband." He told me a lot in that moment but I was too busy trying to fight against it and couldn't just receive it and move forward, without him.

It is dangerous to skip courting and merge right into the relationship lane. If only I had spent time learning about him and had not swan dived right into the bed with this "man of God," then I would have avoided the curse of the Church Playa. You know him. The single man in the church that can pray and always has a word from the Lord. So sanctified and sinful. The man that gives the greatest advice and he's a great listener. The man that rubs your feet and brings you apple juice with no expectation of anything in return, that's him. The fill in boyfriend. The one that you accidentally have sex with and then you two pray about it, however, that doesn't stop you from continuing. I was bamboozled by the appearance of what I thought was holy. Because I had not tapped into discernment, I was going off of my own logic, my own perception.

One evening while I was working late his spiritual sister came into my office and said, "I know you're in love with my brother but he doesn't love you." I was so shocked that my only respond with, "Okay." She went on to tell me that he had not terminated his relationship with his ex-girlfriend and that his family was just happy to have someone else take up the brunt of the responsibility for caring for him. It seemed like he was in tuned with what was happening because he called several times that day and he even showed up to my office, all while she was sitting there serving several blows to my heart. On the ride home I told him what happened and immediately he was infuriated. "Zay, I love you. I'm sorry that you have to go through this and I know being with me isn't easy. Dealing with them and all the other stuff. But I love you and I hope you can see that I love you."

That was the most silent ride home. I looked out of the window and I wondered to myself how I got into this situation.

In May 2011, I was given the opportunity to go to a training with my job for 10 days in Tallahassee. The last week that I was there I was responsible for writing and presenting my own curriculum. While I was in Tallahassee, I noticed that he didn't logoff a social media site on his laptop. I being very inquisitive looked through his mail only to confirm what I knew was true. He was in fact interacting with other women. Being Zay, I decided to change his relationship status to read that he was in a relationship with, Xaviera 'Zay' Bell. Let's just say that this created a mess. When I returned to Jacksonville, he had roses on the dresser awaiting me and he gave me every ounce of the attention that I needed. He helped me with my presentation and was chauffeuring me around town to find a copy center. While in route, he received a telephone call, I could hear the panic from the individual who had contacted him and I knew immediately what it was in reference to. When we arrived home he told me that he needed to talk to me about something. My response was, "So your ex saw that I changed your relationship status. She's upset. Now what?" He was shocked. He started to tell me things about his past and specifically his past with her. I looked at him and asked, "Did you sleep with her when you went to her house when you were supposedly go there to cut ties? That's all I want to know." He looked at me and responded, "Zay." I broke like a dam, the tears flowed and I couldn't even make out what I was saying to him. He held me and said, "I'm so sorry." Between whimpers I said, "But it's me. I would never hurt you. I've never done anything to hurt you. Why? Why would you do this? Why would you damage us?" He had no answers. All he could do was delete his Facebook account in good faith.

As a woman you have an expectation of a man. You have a list of deal breakers and principles that he must possess. But what happens when he breaks all of the deal and possesses only half of the principles and you're still in love. What do you do when you've stayed after all the infidelity and lies? I was in a position where I knew better but I wasn't exemplifying that knowledge of "being in the know". I was standing at the bottom of a pit praying that the love of my life would wake up one day and miraculously become the man that he thought he was; but he didn't.

The months progressed into years and I found myself 4 years involved and clueless about where we were headed. There were talks and plans of marriage but somewhere we became disconnected in our relationship. For several weeks I was clueless as to what was going on and why it was happening. However, on this particular night before we ended our usual telephone conversation he surprised me by saying, "I know that right now it feels strange but trust me it's going to get better. God is doing some things, just be patient. It's going to work out." I couldn't really wrap my head around what he meant but I believed it to be the truth. I was due to arrive in Tampa within the next few days of our conversation and I knew that this was something that we would discuss when I got there.

I was planning to leave by bus, however, God saw fit for me to miss my bus and had to reschedule the trip all together. I left two days later then intended and extended my time there by several days. While in Tampa, I had plans to meet with one of my clients to settle some business that evening. It was very strange that I hadn't heard from him, his phone had been disconnected and I had no way to reach him. After several days I went to his sister's house to stay for the remainder of my time in the city. For the first time I was able to meet his "spiritual mother" face to face. The woman who was not fond of my existence and she clearly wanted nothing to do with me based on what she had heard from others and not by direct contact.

I remember her approaching me while I was peeling apples in the kitchen so that I could make apple turnovers for dinner. She asked if she could talk to me for a moment. I agreed and we took a seat at the dining room table. Surrounded by his family she served me with some news that I was not prepared for. She said, "I hate to be the bearer of bad news but my name is already mud; speaking of herself. I told him if he didn't tell you that I would. He's been married for a year. He got married in Jacksonville and he and his wife live here in Tampa." No one knew it, not even his family. I have never been in a situation where so much pain, grief, and rage met at the same place. I cried. I wept. I pulled up public record just to confirm. There in my face was the truth. He was married on June 24, 2013 to a woman on the other side of town. I sat in silence while tears ran down my face. His spiritual mother says, "See. He decided to marry a real Christian. All the rest of y'all just slept with him. She made him marry her before she jumped in the bed with him. I mean I don't respect any of you because what would you want with a man that doesn't have anything. When a man is avoiding you, you can't make him be with you. When was the last time you even talked to him?" With a tear streaked face I replied, "This morning when he called to tell me that he was coming to see me today." To say she was shocked is an understatement.

His family apologized, hugged me and surrounded me in love like I was related by blood. His sister who had become a really good friend placed her hand on mine and said while in tears, "I am so sorry. You don't deserve this. You deserve so much better." We cried together. That night, I cried myself to sleep. I asked God questions because I needed answers.

The next day he and his wife were no shows to the meeting that we were supposed to have. However, I had advised them previously that he would not show up to face me. Although I didn't know him anymore, somehow I still knew him. Accountability was definitely not his area of strength.

I could still feel the pain as I sat around the dinner table and participated in a prayer that his "spiritual mother" led. I sat there while she prayed for his God ordained marriage, how no decreed that no devil in hell would be able to destroy it. As she poured her heart out in prayer, I recognized that even in ministry she didn't have a heart for everyone, specifically me. I never experienced people face to face who were involved in ministry so pleased at another person's brokenness. Although her story was similar to mine, being deceived by a married man herself, she had no empathy for me.

Later that night, I was pleasantly surprised to see a little girl who had won my heart when she was 2. When she saw me she said, "Hey Mom! I want to sleep with you tonight." How could I say no? Throughout dinner she referred to me as mom and I knew that everyone at the table no longer agreed. I knew that this would be a conversation that would be held later but I didn't care because that's who I had been to her for years. As she lay next to me on the twin sized air mattress she said, "Mom, can me, you, and daddy go to the park?" I said, "Well, daddy and mom aren't friends anymore because daddy has a wife." She looked confused and replied, "So, you and daddy aren't friends anymore because he has a new woman?" In amazement I responded, "Yes."

She shook her head and said, "I'm going to talk to daddy tomorrow and let him know that he married the wrong woman. I'm going to tell him. Daddy, you married the wrong woman, so just marry mom and then we can go to the park and be happy again." As I held her I cried.

The decisions that we make interfere with the lives of others. He didn't think about that when he chose to leave our house, go to the Duval County Courthouse, marry a woman, and come back home to me the same day. We lived in our house for nearly 60 days after he was married and our routine didn't change. We still had dinners together, he still rubbed my feet, he still kissed me, we still had sex every chance that we had. These things ran through my mind on that air mattress. He deceived me and he had cowardly vanished into his existence without even an explanation as to why.

The next morning the daughter of my heart followed me around giving me hugs and kisses. We ate pancakes together and we laughed at any and everything. As I finished my shower I heard her little fist knock on the door. She came into the bathroom and said with tears in her eyes, "Mom, I don't want to go to my daddy's house. I want you to stay here with me." I cried and she cried. I told her, "Mom loves you very much. There are some people that will tell you not to call me mom anymore and I want you to know that this is your choice." She said, "My mom is crying." We hugged and I assured her that I was going to be just fine. The time had come for me to leave. As I gathered my bags I heard her tiny footsteps behind me. Her aunt told her that she couldn't go with us that she would have to stay at the apartment until she returned. With a tremble in her voice she said, "I know. I just want to watch her leave."

I boarded the bus for Orlando and so many thoughts ran through my head. I sat at a smoothie café and tried to gather myself. This was something that was supposed to be happening on a television show, not in my life.

While awaiting the next bus that would take me to Alabama, I received a text message. When I opened it I was shocked to find that it was from him. It read, "I'm sorry. I didn't want it to happen this way." Rage filled my very being. I was sending text messages so rapidly that he called me. Immediately I answered the phone and said, "How dare you! A year? You've been married a year? You let me come here be surrounded by your family. You allowed me to be delivered into the hands of a woman that hates me just to get satisfaction from delivering me a blow like that. You didn't give me the option of whether or not I wanted to be your whore. Why all of this? You just told me that you wanted me to wait for you. I'm talking to you about marriage and you have been married for a year. You have a wife. Why? You were begging for time. Were you planning on getting a divorce?" His response was shocking, "Yes. I asked you to marry me and you rejected me. You told me all the things that I needed to do and I was thinking that if I save up money for a ring I still have to do other things. To marry her was so easy, all I had to do was take her to the courthouse. As soon as I did it I knew that I had made a big mistake."

When I boarded that bus I cried through several counties. I can remember the glass being so cold on my forehead but the tears were so warm rolling down my cheeks. In a matter of moments my life had changed but all I could do was continuously play out this scenario in my head.

By the time I made it to Alabama I had no more tears. I was still grieving because it felt like a death. I contacted him via text and let him know that I needed some answers. He called me and we had a conversation. I cried while I was trying to understand the words that escaped his lips but I couldn't. "What do you want me to do? You've had a year to get used to this but I've only learned about this a few days ago. You changed my life without permission. Do you want this marriage? Do you want ministry?" He replied, "I want ministry."

We had a few conversations via text. Him attempting to manipulate me. Calling me, to tell me that he missed me. Texting me, to tell me that she had left. Advising me that he wasn't in love and that he was buying his time so that he could get out. One day I told him to stop texting me and that the next time we talked it would be face to face.

The pain that I felt during this time I would never wish on any other woman. I cried, I yelled, I was angry. It's scary that a man who professes that he loves the Lord can walk out one day, get married to another woman, and come home like nothing had happened. For 12 months, two weeks, and six days he pretended that he wasn't married. For 12 months, two weeks, and six days he hid his wife from his family. For 12 months, two weeks, and six days he pretended to be a man that loved his fiancé and was preparing for our future and ministry.

A man protects and provides for what he loves. He didn't protect me. He wasn't providing for me. He couldn't love me.

It is so detrimental to the future of women that we don't compromise or sacrifice for men that are not worth it. It doesn't matter how good you are to a person, no matter how much you love them, if they are not loyal, they are just not loyal and you cannot force that. The softer part of us wants to mend and fix them but we never take into consideration that they are probably broken because they have destroyed so many women.

I was so tired of hearing that I deserved better, that he was blocking my ministry; that God had to reveal all of this to me so devastatingly so that I would be done for good. But what about my heart? What was I to do about the damage that he had done to my heart? No words were going to fix the damage. I just had to live through this. I had to pray through this. I had to believe through this.

Have you ever hurt so badly that you thought that your heart would just cease to beat? Your very next breath was labored because you were so grieved and you just wanted the pain to stop, immediately. My mind replayed the events of that moment hundreds of times. I thought back to any clues or indications. What did I miss? Was I that desperate? Was I that lost?

I laid in despair because I couldn't imagine how I was going to walk throughout the journey of my life with someone other than the man that I was desperately in love with. He was supposed to be my partner. He was supposed to love me. He was supposed to be the father of my surviving children. However, he abandoned me, and our dream of building a ministry was something that I couldn't comprehend, see, or cared to visualize. I couldn't eat for days. I wept at night so that no one would see my weakness.

I cried out to God in the darkness of night while everyone else was asleep. Visions of him sleeping next to another female silhouette haunted my thoughts. "God please help me through this," I begged. I knew that this was a journey that I could not walk alone.

While battling all of this in my mind I became physically exhausted. One morning I woke up and decided that I was going to take a walk. With every step joy filled my heart. I started to walk around the community and as I walked God said to me, "It passed over you!" The words were like a lightning bolt through my soul. Then I got it! I put my hands in the air and rejoiced because it could've been me! I could've been caught in a situation with a person that wasn't equipped at the time. I could've been the sacrifice but God said absolutely not, you have a ministry that's in jeopardy. I said, "But I'm feeling different God. Something has changed." He said, "It's okay to have an expiration date on your grieving!"

I was so confused, suddenly I felt different. Don't get me wrong, I was still hurting but I was anticipating the other side of hurt. Healing.

Some of us are still crying over a situation that God saved us from! God says write a date of expiration and on that day your grieving will be over! Count it all joy that it passed over you! You weren't in the plans of demise! It passed over you so that it could position you! Your pain is for a purpose! Your pain is perfecting you! God had to make it better and he didn't want it to be at your expense.

I wish that I could tell you that I went to sleep and I woke up and I didn't love him anymore. I even wished that I could tell you that I never thought about him. I can't do either of those things. But what I can do is tell you that in still loving him, I made a decision to love myself more. I made a choice that when I wake up daily I will choose me and live my best possible life.

Out of all the places for employment that I applied for Tampa was the only city that returned my calls. I am employed with a company that I love, making more money than I had made in my career; all while living less than 10 miles from him. The bitter sweet journey that we call life. The hurtful, tumultuousness of this journey. How can a place that caused me so much pain produce so much fruit? Know your soil! Sometimes things have to be dug out and the soil has to be plowed to mix some things up. That is what Tampa has become to me, new fertile ground.

Know this. Know that life doesn't always happen how we plan in our heads. Know that we will get bumps and bruises. Know that we will hurt and have a good face contorting cry and its okay. But ultimately know. YOU'RE A BIG DEAL. And if no one else recognizes that, you embed it in your mind, your heart, your every breath, and your DNA. Because you're worth it.

Wake up every day and choose you. You're just that wonderful!

www.ingramcontent.com/pod-product-compliance
Lightning Source LLC
Chambersburg PA
CBHW060459090426
42735CB00011B/2047